HUGO MACDONALD is a design, architecture and urbanism critic and consultant living in London. He studied Arabic and modern history at Cambridge University before moving to London. He was deputy editor of *Wallpaper** magazine's website and then design editor at *Monocle* magazine, where he hosted *Monocle* radio's weekly design and architecture show, *Section D*. After a stint as the brand director at Studioilse, Ilse Crawford's design consultancy, today he has his own company. His writing has been published in titles including the *Financial Times*, the *Guardian*, *Modern Design Review* and the *Journal of the London Society*.

THE SCHOOL OF LIFE is dedicated to exploring life's big questions: *How do we find fulfilling work? Can we ever understand our past? Why are relationships so hard to master? If we could change the world, should we?* Based in London, with campuses around the globe, The School of Life offers classes, therapies, books and other tools to help you create a more satisfying life. We don't have all the answers but we will direct you towards a variety of ideas from the humanities – from philosophy to literature, psychology to the visual arts – guaranteed to stimulate, provoke, nourish and console.

How to Live in the City
Hugo Macdonald

MACMILLAN

First published 2016 by Macmillan
an imprint of Pan Macmillan
20 New Wharf Road, London N1 9RR
Associated companies throughout the world
www.panmacmillan.com

ISBN 978-1-4472-9331-6

9 8 7 6 5 4 3 2 1

A CIP catalogue record for this book is
available from the British Library.

Typeset by seagulls.net

Printed and bound by CPI Group (UK) Ltd,
Croydon, CR0 4YY

Visit **www.panmacmillan.com** to
read more about all our books and to
buy them. You will also find features,
author interviews and news of any
author events, and you can sign up for
e-newsletters so that you're always first
to hear about our new releases.

For Skye and London, Mum and Dad, and James

Contents

Introduction

Can I see myself here?

'Being human is itself difficult, and therefore all kinds of settlements have problems. Big cities have difficulties in abundance, because they have people in abundance.'

(JANE JACOBS, *THE DEATH AND LIFE OF GREAT AMERICAN CITIES*)

Being Human, Not Feral

This is a book about being human in the city. As Jane Jacobs, one of the greatest urban writers and thinkers of modern times, puts it so beautifully, 'being human is itself difficult'. Being human together in large numbers is extremely difficult. Being human in the city is a challenge. And that, presumably, is why you are holding this book. It is a book to help with the challenges we face living in the city. It is a book to help you feel human in an inhuman environment.

Living in a city changes our faculties. Just as it can heighten our sense of awe and joy, so too can it damage our senses, sensibility and sense of judgement. City living can make and break us in the same week, day or even hour. It can warp us to the point that we become something other than ourselves. Take an average daily commute in rush hour as proof that even the most civilized of humans can quickly descend into feral behaviour when locked in a crowd or pressed up close against an unfragrant armpit.

There is, of course, far more pleasure to be derived from life in the city than the odd horrible train journey. But as cities grow (and almost all cities are growing), systems, services and resources are continuously pushed to their limits, and the trials and tribulations of daily urban life are consequently increasing too. How can we ensure that the good doesn't get engulfed by the bad?

Against the backdrop of this swollen urban reality, there's an absence of handbooks for surviving, coping or nurturing our love for day-to-day living in cities. Tourist guidebooks, physical and virtual, are churned out at a rate of knots. But there's a distinct lack of books that tell us how to live in our own cities, how to cope with the rush and the crush, the grit and the grime. This is the mission of the book you are reading.

My love of city life is at odds with – or perhaps more accurately, a reaction to – my upbringing, which could not have been more rural. I grew up in a place called Sleat, on the Isle of Skye, off the north-west coast of Scotland. Our home was a small hotel run by my parents in a spectacular setting at the foot of a mountain, in front of a sea loch. It was down a forestry track, over a bridge a few kilometres from the single-track road that connected us to the nearest settlements on the island. Back then, Skye was still an island (the bridge connecting it to the mainland came in 1995). It was remote, and almost always rainy.

As a child my impressions of the city were gathered from snatches of news bulletins on TV, newspaper headlines and photographs together with stories and an odd collection of ephemera we had lying around. It was the 1980s. Cities were filled with police, riots and car bombs. We had a board game called 'Ratrace' with the dubious tagline, 'the game the social climbers play'. It was a boom-and-bust money game that brashly encouraged its players to buy their way through life with greasy ease. In my curious mind, London was dangerous, evil and full of rats climbing over each other to get ahead.

When I was seven we went to visit my aunt who lived down there, and the scales fell from my eyes. I was hooked. We didn't see any riots, and thankfully no car bombs either. That said, my sister was so anxious about the IRA she was sick into my aunt's cutlery drawer (incidentally, she lives back in Skye today). But what we did see was a world unlike anything I had previously imagined. There were giant mechanical billboards that showed three adverts in succession; black taxis; black people; Indian people; Chinese people; strange pink Chinese food hanging in windows; policemen on horses; the BT Tower; haircuts like works of art; piercings and make-up on women and men. It was so big, messy, dirty, busy. All of it was new to me, and thrilling. The energy was an awakening, to say the least. I think of that first trip often. It helps in times when I'm tired of the hassle of city life to remember how impressed I once was by the scale, the action and the pace. It helps me to pause, take a deep breath and let the awe inspire me all over again.

So Who Is this Book For?

The short answer is that this book is for anybody who lives in a city. A more considered answer would be that it's for anybody who recognizes any of the following feelings or statements:

- I feel awkward that I don't know anything about the life of the man who gives me coffee each morning.
- I'd love to see that exhibition/concert/play/film; I must make time for it. Another weekend gone and I've got nothing to show for it but a hangover.
- Dammit, I missed that exhibition. Am I the only person that didn't see it?
- Why are people intent on standing still, in front of me, when I'm in a hurry?
- I don't see enough of my friends; why is it so difficult to arrange anything with them?
- Why do I dread doing things or having any plans?
- Hooray – they cancelled on me, and now I have an evening to myself.
- Is it normal to feel irrational anger towards so many strangers on a daily basis?
- There is so much food on these shelves, and yet I can't find anything I want.
- I'm unhappy with my job/partner/friends/apartment, but I don't have the energy right now to find a new one. Where do you even start looking?
- I want to be the person who is running at 9:30 a.m. on a Saturday; why am I still in bed? Again? And now it's midday, and I'm thirty-three, and still in bed.
- I tell my friends and family I love this city because there's so much to do here. But if I'm honest, I feel bad because I never do any of it.

- Who was it that said if you're tired of London, you're tired of life? Maybe I should try New York. Maybe I should move to the seaside. And who said that only boring people feel bored? Does that mean I'm boring, or tired of life? Or both? How could this happen when I live in London?

If any of these feelings strikes the smallest chord of recognition, then there is something in this book for you.

The Art of a Relationship

Living in a city is an art, not a science. Choosing to live in a city is choosing to enter into a relationship with it. And, like any human relationship, the relationship you have with your city is one that requires nurturing, constant practice and work. How can you be conscious, not unconscious? How can you feel, instead of being numb? How can you be active, not passive? When should you be hard and when should you be soft? When should you fight and when should you be still? What should you take and how can you give back? We will address each of these questions in depth over the following chapters.

London is where I call home, though this book will draw from a well of experiences spanning a decade of intense travel to nearly 150 cities around the world. As a journalist writing about design, architecture and urbanism, I was lucky enough to have doors opened frequently by many people to many places that gave me great insight to the cities I travelled to. I was careful to try to sample 'real life' (whatever that means) wherever possible, and swerve the constructed impression that city-hall officials or tourist boards might have preferred me to leave with. I made friends along the way – and these friends' experiences, together with my own, form much of the primary source material of this book. If there is a bias towards London, forgive me; it is in part because this is where so many of my thoughts have been cultivated. It is also because, under the microscope of urban living, London is one of the world's greater Petri dishes. So much that is said about London life can be applied to many other cities, regardless of culture or climate, geography or scale.

I don't think I'm alone, in London or any city, in finding myself harassed on the flesh jigsaw of the underground at rush hour or guilt-ridden about the number of things I'd like to do that I never get round to. Yet still the city thrills me. The opportunities, the energy and the unending sense of possibility are gripping. It makes me feel alive. I'm learning and practising how to feel good, not guilty. And how to feel, full stop. I'm learning how to slow down, and when to speed up. I am by no means a model of virtue. But, where once upon a time I despaired at the grimness of passing out on the night bus and waking up in an overlit suburban bus depot, today I let myself off more often. Or just get a taxi.

It is by living through trying, exploring and sharing experiences that we accrue valuable insight into what works (and doesn't) for us as individuals living in cities. After all, being human is being individual. The more we take ownership and responsibility of ourselves as individuals within the city, the more likely we are to find our own individual places, comfortably, within it.

People in Cities

We are all constantly bombarded with statistics regarding urban growth. When someone tells us anecdotally that by 2050, 75 per cent of the world's population will live in cities, we are no longer flabbergasted. We have been numbed by overexposure to facts and consequences via a flood of TV shows, columns, bestsellers, conferences, photos, lists, shares, likes. So saturated are we by the language of urbanism that we have become detached from what it really means and how it impacts us. Trying to understand the future of our cities has somehow become separated from understanding what happens to us, the inhabitants of these ever-changing cities. The city as an abstract entity has become the foreground and we, its human inhabitants, have become the backdrop. When it comes to talking about happiness, it is personal, human experience that really counts.

This is not a book about urbanism; it is a book about how people live in cities, and for people living in cities. It is a book that seeks to share, through experience, observation and common sense, the potential for our healthy growth as humans living together in an urban environment. It is about the peculiar situations and circumstances that we find ourselves in: what makes us help a stranger to their feet in a station ticket hall, and then cross the road to avoid saying hello to a friend?

It is a widely held belief that in order to live happily in a city you need to be rich. There is no denying that money (or not having to worry about it) increases one's quality of life generally, but as we are all increasingly aware, it is by no means the answer to all of our woes. Human values count for more, and they cost nothing when it comes to inner peace and outer fulfilment. Some of the more dismal experiences I've had of late have been in soulless, expensive restaurants and hotels I'd often imagined would be the pinnacle of living – instead, everything there (including most of the people) seemed empty, awkward and curiously out of date.

The book is divided into five chapters, each of which takes a different aspect of city living and suggests how you might make the most of it. We begin with the question of how to find your place within the city: how to meet and greet it and build a relationship with it on your own terms. The second chapter deals with the relationships we have with other city dwellers, from casual acquaintances to friends and partners – and, crucially, the relationship we have with ourselves. Chapter Three is about finding that all-important work/life balance: when and how to play, and when and how to focus on work without grazing your nose too hard on the grindstone and exploding with stress. In Chapter Four we look at how to move around the city: that's everything from being early to getting lost, using the city for exercise and the joy of talking to taxi drivers. The final chapter is about how to give back to the city: how to feed it and help it grow.

It is a handbook, rather than a textbook or guidebook. My hope is that it will help you to think about how and why we behave, respond or feel (or don't) in a certain way in cities. With any luck, it will encourage you to try behaving, responding or feeling more like a human being, and less like a cog in a machine. It stands to reason that the more human we all strive to be and to feel, the more humane our urban environments will be.

1. How to Feel Your City

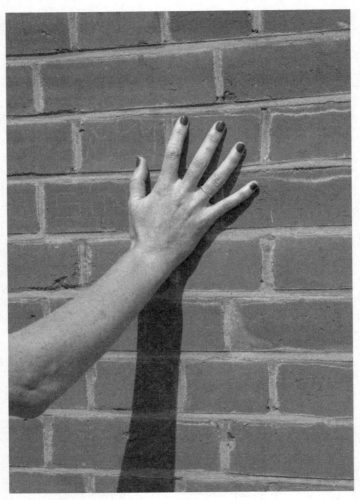

What does the city feel like?

'The soul of the city is that part of it which is of no value from the practical side of existence: it is quite simply its poetry, a feeling which in itself is absolute, though it is so definitely a part of ourselves.'

(LE CORBUSIER, *THE CITY OF TO-MORROW AND ITS PLANNING*)

Shaking Hands with Your City

The first step to forming a good relationship with the city you live in is to introduce yourself to it, and vice versa – just like a human relationship. This is an exercise in understanding what your city is about, what it stands for, what its values are and how they have been formed. It also helps you to find where you fit into it. I call this 'feeling the city'.

Asking people whether they understood what I meant when I spoke of feeling a city, I was surprised how varied their responses were. They ranged from the pragmatic – mastering the underground system, or walking instead of taking public transport – to the cultural: reading a canon of literature from the city's past, or tapping into its musical heritage. And then there are the less quantifiable sensory measures. By this, I mean physical engagement with the city you live in. Go to a building or monument, one that speaks to you personally rather than the obvious landmarks that you might find on a postcard (though these are fine too, if you connect with them beyond finding them merely 'iconic'). Touch it with flat palms. Stroke it with your eyes closed. Try to feel it and think about the city as a whole through this sensation. It might sound daft, but there is truth to the idea that buildings, and indeed cities as a whole, are repositories of energy and memory.

What will you feel? It is a symbolic gesture, really: an act of dedicating time to focus and think, aided by the sense of touch. It is like sitting on a bench with an inscription to someone you do not know, which nevertheless makes you feel something. It is a way of bringing the city, a giant intangible mass of history, culture, buildings and people, into your hand and feeling it physically; and also, perhaps, emotionally. It reduces the scale to something more manageable. It is literally like shaking hands with the city. For me, I find it works better with older buildings made of stone, marble or brick, where you can soak up the history through responsive materials that show their age through the wear and tear of years. But even the cold sheen of a glass curtain wall can return something interesting.

Touching buildings has awakened my love for several cities. Rome springs to mind instantly – a place where you can touch buildings (and fragments of them) that predate Christianity. You can literally feel history, and it is humbling. Climbing over monumental marble fragments of imperial Roman buildings in the Forum brought the past to life for me. Helsinki is another city to which I was awakened through touch; the solid, rugged buildings, designed to withstand the severest of winters, have a comforting, gentle roughness to them that is reassuring, much like the Finns themselves. In New York I'm fascinated by the edges of buildings in Manhattan, the right angle at which the grid turns, casting bright daylight into darkness. Man versus nature.

When asked about the feelings urban living evokes, people often respond that the city overwhelms them. It's no surprise, given the crush and the speed, the relentlessness and the difficulty of carving out time for respite. Feeling the city you live in is a very handy exercise in slowing down and connecting; establishing a sense of belonging, a small, tangible sense of ownership. A root.

Finding Your City's Values

In recent decades cities have been hijacked by brand and marketing brigades, which makes establishing a genuine connection with your own city a little trickier. Through billboards, adverts, slogans and an avalanche of merchandise we are told our city is one thing, and yet our own experiences are often very different. The disparity can be confusing.

The city you live in is not a brand. It might be presented as such to attract developers, businesses, foreign investors and tourists, but the relationship you have with your city as an inhabitant needs to be more personal than an image derived from a billboard, or the stereo-typed tat sold in a gift shop. You will understand Edinburgh better if you run your hands over the sharp, crenellated Scott Monument than if you buy a tam-o'-shanter with a ginger wig attached. The marketing slogan 'Incredinburgh' doesn't really do it justice either. I've never

been to Wellington, and 'Absolutely Positively Wellington' does little
to inspire me to visit.

Understanding the values of a city requires research and time,
but is definitely worth the effort. By values, I mean: what does the city
stand for? What are its particular qualities? If it were a person, how
would you describe its character? What is its 'soul', as Le Corbusier
would say, made up of?

The answers lie somewhere in the intersection between history,
culture, topography and climate, with certain cities pulled in certain
directions more or less than others. It's a sense you get from a mixture
of people and place. Cities of former imperial nations tend to carry
the bombast with them still, be that in the scale of their buildings,
the width of their streets (all the better for processions) or the hint
of blustering confidence that remains in the population. London,
Paris, Lisbon, Madrid, Vienna, Rome, Berlin, Istanbul – European
capital cities excel here. By contrast, the mighty industrial American
cities look, work and feel like machines. The younger Asian cities feel
more transient and digital, bearing the hallmarks of computer-aided
architecture and urban planning. The even younger Emirati cities
feel unreal, dystopian and mesmerizing in their towering ambitions,
like mirages in the sand.

These generalizations are a starting point, a backdrop or frame-
work to dig deeper and uncover the idiosyncrasies that lie at the heart
of the city you live in. These values speak to us as individuals. When I
compare what I understand London's values to be with a friend, they
can differ widely based on how we conduct our individual relationships with the city, what we choose to see and what we leave behind.
To me, London is stoic. It is hermetic and hard (albeit with a few

soft bits). It is modest and proud, though maybe not as proud as Paris. It is fairly rigid and old-fashioned, but plucky. I think of it as a curmudgeonly, domineering old relative filled with stories. I feel these qualities in unexpected places: in derelict buildings, rows of Victorian terraces and even in sad, new developments. I feel it in a soggy rush hour and on the packed street outside a pub in the evening sunlight. I recognize these qualities in Charles Dickens' vision of London, and also in Samuel Pepys' diaries. I see it in the paintings of Monet and Turner and I hear it in the music of the Kinks and the Rolling Stones; gritty, uncomfortable, yet paradoxically comforting and charming at the same time. This, for me, is London.

You need to define what the city you live in represents and what it stands for in your opinion. Only then can you embark on working out where you fit in. It's crucial that you bring something of yourself to the city, but I think a sense of humility is appropriate here too. As with most things, striking a balance is key: don't be so timid that you let the city fill you up like an empty vessel, but equally, don't enter into a relationship with the city with the intention of changing it to suit you. Find your niche. Locate the sides of your city's character that you respond to, and cherish them. You are sowing seeds that will grow into a sense of belonging to your city, which in turn develops into a sense of ownership.

In a nutshell this process is a method of applying emotional intelligence to your relationship with your city. I'm surprised by the number of people I speak to who regard the city as an inanimate, passive entity, something they would never have thought to try to embark on a relationship with. They might acknowledge that some-times the city gets them down and sometimes lifts them up, but they have not realized that they have the keys to these responses, or that it's in their power to nurture and enhance this relationship. As Edward Glaeser says in his book *Triumph of the City*, 'We must free ourselves from our tendencies to see cities as buildings and remember that the real city is made of flesh, not concrete.'

A Sense of Place

After stressing the need to bring your city down to a manageable scale in order to have a relationship with it, it sounds contradictory to recommend you find a spot where you can see as much of the city as possible. But do it and visit it regularly. Cities are awesome in the real sense of the word, and being frequently awe-inspired by your habitat is a good thing. It helps you to gain perspective; it helps you to remember that your environment is larger than the sum of you and your own existence, your worries, your hopes and fears. Just as it helps to feel and understand the city on your terms, so it helps to be humbled by it too. There is a reason why so many films set in cities include sweeping helicopter shots of the urban landscape. Parisians might hate it (to the extent they banned buildings over a certain height after it was built), but I defy anyone not to feel moved by the view over Paris from the roof of the Tour Montparnasse. You don't have to find a tall building, though, let alone get into a helicopter – in fact, I find views across or out, rather than down, easier to connect to a cityscape. (The Danish urban pioneer Jan Gehl made a wonderful illustration that shows the increasing detachment of humans from real life, the higher the storey of their building.)

In London, I go to Nunhead Cemetery, one of the great Victorian cemeteries. Nunhead is in a sad state of disrepair, and nowhere near as manicured as its more famous sister up in Highgate. But this only adds to the atmosphere. Climbing through the rubbled graves and monuments, in varied states of surrender to the ivy and undergrowth, you emerge from the woods onto a small hill with a bench. And in the clearing there is a wonderful view down and over the City of London, with St Paul's framed in the centre. The surprise of this view is breathtaking, and it conjures up feelings that go beyond mere nostalgia. At this spot, I feel London intensely.

> The world is full of cities and towns constantly growing larger. But the people within them are less connected. Yet we are all yearning for a sense of place. We are all seeking to belong. We all want to connect and share. To feel accepted and feel safe. Imagine having that anywhere. Airbnb stands for something much bigger than travel. We imagine a world where you can belong anywhere.
>
> (AIRBNB PROMOTIONAL FILM)

For humans, connection to place is a profoundly important part of our existential identity. It helps us to feel that we matter, and that we are able to make our mark, or be marked in some way by something bigger than ourselves. The British journalist and cultural commentator Jonathan Meades has a wonderful way of bringing a sense of place to life. He is sardonic and insightful in equal measure. His documentaries and writing cut through description to bring fact, culture and emotional intelligence together in one. His work is not to everyone's liking, and he has as many critics as fans, but more than anyone, he has opened my eyes to a way of acutely feeling a sense of place.

I feel that a connection to place is more important now than ever, as we increasingly outsource so much of our lives to the intangible and invisible in the technology that so many of us rely on. On moving from Skye to London, I was struck how my friends who had grown up in the city spoke of their relationships to it. For me, connection to place had always been rooted in nature and landscape. Their connection was more abstract; it was related to the soul of the city, which was man-made and largely concrete but no less emotive for its lack of nature. As a non-native urban dweller it has taken time for me to equate the strong tug I feel towards the mountains and lochs of Skye with the cityscape, which once upon a time seemed so cold, transient and man-made by comparison. Can you love a building in the same way that you love a mountain? The answer is yes.

Can I Be Myself Here?

For anyone moving to a city for the first time, choosing a neighbourhood, street, building and floor is your first step to making yourself at home. This requires patience and a cool head: two things I am not blessed with. In twelve years of London living I have lived in ten different flats, and one boat. This nomadic life has been partly the result of circumstance, and partly of choice. I get restless, and I'm not convinced I've yet found the place where I really want to nest. For those already living in the city – presumably the majority of readers –

it is likely you have moved around, too. As our circumstances develop and change, so do our requirements for a home. Finding a place where we feel settled is crucial not just to our physical well-being, but our emotional and even mental health too. Being homeless is a destabilizing horror far beyond not having a roof over your head.

Whether buying or renting, my friends who have settled upon a location hold a common view on the subject, which boils down to one question: do you feel like yourself in this neighbourhood and street? It's hardly an earth-shattering revelation, but the more I thought about it and poked around the process, the more I understood its valuable nuances. All cities are made up of neighbourhoods and communities with unique characters and atmospheres. These change as places fall in and out of favour with certain groups. Some places gentrify. Some places go to seed. It's the ongoing cycle of urban growth, renewal and decay. Jane Jacobs wrote extensively about the importance of having a mixed community for a healthy neighbourhood. And she was right. When cities become socially fragmented, problems arise. As soon as a community becomes too singular it turns into a ghetto, and ghettos aren't healthy for cities or their inhabitants.

More important than trying to engineer a mix with your presence, however, is working out whether you feel comfortable as a member of this community – and comfortably anonymous within it, too. Do you feel normal here? It's not so much about hunting for like-minded groups of people, but rather feeling a resonance with the people and place. 'Fitting in' sounds so dull and passive, but when it comes to your neighbourhood, sticking out is worse.

But how are you supposed to read a neighbourhood? Sadly you cannot test-drive a flat or house. One friend said she spent a long

Am I comfortable here?

time in the local supermarket, from where she was able to see a cross-section of the community in how shoppers and staff spoke to each other. She scoured the local message boards, which told her there were more music teachers in the area than Hell's Angels, and she was sold. It's a good tactic, and I'd expand on it by setting aside a day at the very least to sample pubs, cafes and restaurants or even just to sit on a bench and observe. You'll be surprised at how much you can pick up about a street or neighbourhood when you actively watch, rather than just passively see. It's more knowledge and insight than you'll get from an estate agent, for whom every area is forever 'on the up'.

All Talk

Our cities speak to us, and to a certain extent they tell us how to live in them. Street signage has a great impact on how we read our cities. Visiting cities where the language is so alien you can't even guess at what the signage might say can leave you feeling lost, physically and emotionally – though it can be thrilling too.

It amazes me how the character of different cities is expressed through street signage. American cities are fond of blunt impera-tives: 'walk' and 'don't walk'. You know where you stand (and you know when to move). The signage is graphic, filmic, considered, constant. American cities talk to you; they move quickly, and they want you to be in the right place at the right time. The London we currently live in tells you off a lot. There are endless signs telling you what you're forbidden from doing: 'no radios in the park', 'no dogs', 'no food', 'no cameras'. We are in danger of feeling cowed into having no fun.

I've always loved Berlin's *Ampelmännchen* pedestrian man: one of the few gifts from the days when communist East Berlin was walled off from the West, this perky, hatted little chap strides confidently in green and stands to attention when red. He lends the city a subtle layer of charm. The Rome I've always loved for allowing me to stroke its ruins and feel its past is in danger of becoming a museum city thanks to the preservation police, who have hung '*non toccare*' ('don't touch') signs in abundance.

We are surrounded in cities by signs, notices, calls to action and calls to halt. Consider what their tone is, and how they make you feel. Should we listen, or should we touch anyway?

Where Does It Start?

I became a fully fledged London citizen myself in 2003. I arrived from university with all my possessions in two suitcases and moved into a ground-floor flat in Camden Square for six weeks, charged with looking after it while its owner went travelling. Prior to this I had stayed with my sisters and friends in the city for weeks at a time, but this move felt different and significant, albeit temporary. London was now my home. Previous visits were like courting or dating, and now we were in a relationship.

I was living by myself and had a lot of time to think about things, helped by the fact that the television didn't work and I didn't have a computer. I listened to the radio, I read, I cooked and I cleaned. It was therapeutic – until I found a giant house spider in the bath. Being severely arachnophobic, I was paralysed with fear. As I hovered over it with a towel for what seemed like forever, I felt totally inept and lacking. Try as I might to muster the courage of Robert the Bruce in his cave, when faced with a spider I was clearly made of less sterling stuff.

Spiders aside, being in the city felt liberating and scary at the same time. London didn't feel like home instantly; I felt like I was play-acting living there. I longed for months to pass, for things to feel normal and familiar, routine and easy. I had my wallet stolen. My journey from the tube to the front door took me past two rowdy pubs filled with swaying, shouting drunk men. I dreaded the walk after dark. The quieter streets off the main road felt even more menacing. I felt conspicuous, fragile and homesick for more carefree days in smaller places, where you could bump into people in the street and be the master of your own destiny.

I was struck in those early days by the constant noise and smell of the city. Even if I did ever manage to fit into it, I felt it would be impossible to bring anything of myself to it. It was so much bigger and more defined than I was; it engulfed me entirely.

Feeling insignificant is a fundamentally depressing prospect. So how do you begin to feel empowered by something so much greater than you? It comes in small steps. For me, it began with realizing my neighbours were sociable and fun. The steps of the house I lived in were the perfect place to have coffee and a cigarette in the mornings in the late autumn sunshine. There was a small public garden nearby. A bus could take me past the scary pubs at night. And actually they weren't so scary after all, as open-mic karaoke nights soon proved. Bit by bit I found my feet and felt comfortable with my place. It was less about giving in or succumbing, and more about making it work for me. It's easy to feel scared of the unknown, but there are small steps you can take to demystify an alien environment: talk to the people who run your local shop; build up a routine that makes you visible in your local cafe, gym, pub; look online to find any community initiatives that you might be interested in getting involved with.

I often think back to those first six weeks to remind myself, when things seem insurmountable, of where my relationship with the city started. It's important to recognize that it keeps on growing.

Making a Routine

Whether we like to admit it or not, we are all creatures of habit. Routine is comforting and secure. It is a mark of civilization and speaks of order, of purpose, of control, of the self-actualization at the top of Maslow's hierarchy of needs. And yet (or maybe because of these associations) it can also feel stifling. There is a sequence in Tim Burton's film *Edward Scissorhands* in which Bill Boggs leaves his house for work in the morning. He gets into his car, reverses out of the drive and into the road . . . at which point the camera pans up to show the entire identikit suburban population going through exactly the same routine. It is beautiful as a piece of theatre, but disturbing in its implications. The problem with routine is that it doesn't tend to allow for the joys of spontaneity, or serendipity, or individualism.

Having a routine in the city is necessary to provide you with structure in relation to the city and the other inhabitants. It establishes order amid the chaos. Finding a balance is everything. There is no point in a routine so comprehensive that it leaves no room for flexibility, else you will set yourself up for repeated disappointment; but you do need enough triggers to create a daily sense of familiarity. Establishing this is an important part of carving out your patch, another tool for feeling a sense of belonging and ownership in the city.

An appropriate level of routine is something you work out for yourself by trial and error over time. Much of it is better described as ritual than routine – ritual is a more weighted word which, in turn, gives reassuring weight to our lives. There is a solemnity associated with a sequence of actions undertaken in a particular order. You don't have to be religious to appreciate the benefits of bringing ritual into your life, of course, but there is a spiritual aspect to it: it is practising the art of slowing down, of stepping outside yourself a little rather than speeding unconsciously through the day. The Danish word '*hygge*', though difficult to translate directly, incorporates ritual, generosity, a sense of calm and an appreciation of beauty. It refers to the importance of small moments embedded in Danish culture and daily life, like lighting a candle in the mornings to ease your transition into the day.

I have learnt a great deal about this aspect of life from my mentor and former employer, the designer Ilse Crawford. She places great importance on the value that daily rituals bring to our sense of well-being. Where possible and appropriate, she takes these ordinary actions and moments and upgrades them either with specific objects (such as the collection of everyday vessels and containers she designed for Georg Jensen) or framing them spatially with considered materials, furniture and lighting, in the residential and public spaces she designs. The result is that the ordinary becomes something extraordinary; small moments of joy on a daily basis, in place of the humdrum or mundane.

Routine, regime, habit and ritual can mean all manner of things in the context of the city. It's the time you set your alarm; the sequence of your ablutions; any exercise you might take; breakfast; your route to work; frequenting the same coffee venue, and so on. It is the behavioural pattern that we all adhere to, often to the extent that it becomes mechanical. We don't question it. Do we even enjoy it? Does it suit us? Suddenly days have rolled into weeks, months into years, and we've become hamsters on a wheel.

As important as it is to have structure, it is equally important to break free from it. Think about your routine, and think about how and when you can shake it up. Try getting up an hour earlier and walking to work instead of taking public transport. Experiment with a different route to open your eyes to a different side of the city. Go out for breakfast with your partner or friends. I'm not suggesting you throw your routine out the window for good; it's important for your stability and sanity, even, that it remains nearly intact. But breaking it tactically, frequently, makes it mean something. It will allow you to stay conscious, active and alert, and help prevent the routine from taking over and lulling you into the malaise of autopilot mode.

Am I Missing Out?

The fear of missing out – or FOMO, as today's acronym-obsessed text generation might have it – is a common symptom of city living. It manifests itself in a number of ways, reflecting your perceptions

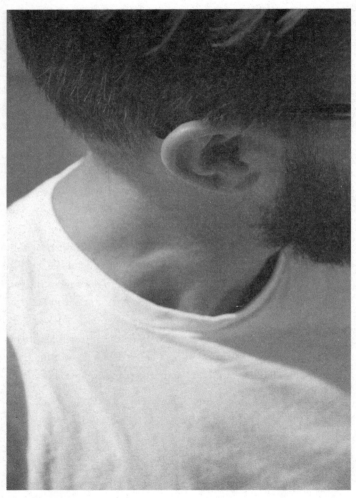

Am I missing out?

of how integrated into the city you feel, or how much you fret over all that you can't keep up with.

We have all had friends or colleagues who talk incessantly about the new, or next, best thing. The pop-up restaurant that everyone's raving about, the exhibition with queues around the block, the club night that only lets in the fifty best dressed people, the sell-out theatre performance, the flash sale, the secret book-swap carnival, the inflatable boat parade. It's like a thinly veiled competition about who has their finger more firmly on the city's pulse, who is doing more, who is using their time to their maximum. And it can be anxiety-inducing, even when you've actively chosen not to do something.

Our obsession with the next best thing and the activities of others is a blight of our consumer-driven society, and it is felt most keenly in cities. It is up to us to quiet the voice inside that asks why we always feel late to the party. The truth is that there will always be so much more happening in a city than you can ever spread yourself across, in person or even in awareness. We will always be surrounded by more different things we can possibly do. It is the difficulty of choice when faced with such a glut of opportunity that feels paralysing. Making decisions is scary, and yet being confident in the decisions we make is the key to so much happiness and fulfilment in life. The word 'decision' originates from the Latin *de* and *caedere*, meaning to cut off – literally slaying your options. It's learning when and what to opt in and out of that really matters, though. Have confidence in your choices: make sure that they reflect who you are, and what you enjoy. Don't succumb to peer pressure, or let yourself become a wingman in someone else's experience of city life. And don't end up doing nothing because you couldn't decide what to do.

Planning ahead is a useful strategy in combating FOMO. Set dates to do things, book tickets for shows, concerts and tables at restaurants. Invite others to join you. This is a simple way of ensuring you will have things in your diary to look forward to. Engineer your own fun, and take others along for the ride; we all love the friends who are organized enough to book tickets in bulk and bring everyone together. Just be mindful of scheduling sufficient space for spontaneity too.

Feeling Safe

It is easy to believe that cities are dangerous. We are exposed to news reports and statistics that can terrify timid souls into thinking every stranger on the sidewalk is a criminal in waiting. Clearly crime is more prevalent in cities than in rural areas, but much of this is due to the greater concentration of people. It is vital not to be intimidated into living under the covers for fear of what might happen. Feeling safe is largely a matter of common sense and vigilance: the more vigilant we are as city inhabitants, the stronger we become together as a deterrent. In general, it makes sense to keep to places where there are other people.

And just as being alert to your own safety is common sense, be aware of the safety of others too. If you happen to witness an incident, act with courage but caution. We've all heard the parable of the woman who was attacked on the street in broad daylight in front of many people, but no one intervened because they assumed someone else would. Should any of us find ourselves the unfortunate victim in such a situation, a good way to attract help is to shout out to someone individually, referring to them by what they are wearing, thereby giving them ownership of the situation and responsibility to act.

It is important to foster your own feelings of safety. Don't put yourself in situations where you feel unsafe. Make connections with people in your neighbourhood. Be active and alert, not passive or invisible. As a city dweller you have a responsibility to be part of a community that looks out for its other members. We are all in it together.

Feeling Clean

Cities are dirty. Even the more clinical, manicured Mitteleuropean or Japanese cities have cars, and pollution, and inhabitants with germs who don't wash their hands and occasionally sneeze on the back of your neck. For anyone even moderately concerned with hygiene, urban living is a constant battle the moment you leave the sanctity of your own home.

The grime of pollution is tough. Blowing your nose after a journey on any underground transport system is not a pretty sight, and imagining what's in your lungs after a day out on foot or bike is enough to induce panic. Unfortunately, dirty air is a trade-off we have to accept in return for the many pleasures of city living. Short of buying a respiratory mask, there's little you can do to shield yourself from pollution. Things are looking up, though. Fewer cars on the streets means less pollution in the air, and thankfully most cities are on board with the idea that this is the way forward. Most of us can take small comfort from knowing that things are better today than they were for our forebears, who could almost chew what they inhaled.

When it comes to germs, we all fall foul of the inconsistent and selfish habits of humankind. Despite all the advice to wash our hands, catch a sneeze in a tissue and so forth, all it takes is one rogue individual not playing along to ruin it for everyone. It's easy to be too precious. It took me years to pluck up the courage to hold a handrail on public transport. I became a master of pulling my jumper sleeve over my hand in situations when I had to hold on, and I washed my jumpers frequently. Tales of norovirus taking down whole train carriages did nothing to quell my anxiety, and films like *Outbreak* and *Contagion*, with scenes that show the vast spreading of a sneeze in a public space, only compounded my fear. I clocked up hours washing my hands with reassuringly blue antibacterial hand wash.

I wouldn't say I suffered from OCD – more an irrational fear of germs and illness. It didn't limit what I could do, but it did make for an unhealthy mistrust of my neighbouring citizens, to the point where I could muster up hatred for sneezers at close quarters. I didn't enjoy travelling, and being out in public generally made me hyper-aware of hazardous toilet door handles, bowls of shared nuts at the bar and discarded newspapers. On more paranoid days, being out and about in the city felt difficult and stressful. I felt out of control.

Then I read Suellen M. Hoy's book *Chasing Dirt: The American Pursuit of Cleanliness*, which documents our modern obsession with cleanliness. Much of our anxiety was born from (and nurtured by) the strategic alliance of the burgeoning industries surrounding sanitaryware and soap in the early twentieth century. Their marketing exploited society's preoccupation with questions around immigration, ethnic segregation, snobbery and social climbing. Think of the implications behind the phrase 'Cleanliness is next to godliness'. I gave myself a stern talking to and adjusted my thinking. Living in a mild yet constant state of fear of the unknown unclean is a waste of emotional energy. I wouldn't go so far as to say I now love my sneezing neighbours, but I am far more tolerant. I don't hate them irrationally any more; I don't change train carriages to escape every spluttering cougher. I hold handrails. I still wash my hands at any opportunity, but my phobia of germs has subsided. Perhaps my immune system has even strengthened as a result. If these anxieties ring true to you, try converting contempt into compassion by thinking of your fellow urban dwellers as human neighbours rather than walking germs. Tolerance is such a vital part of city living, and learning how to tolerate our proximity to each other is key to living comfortably together. No one really chooses to be ill, and the majority of us are gracious enough when ill not to actively seek to spread our germs.

In our pandemic-obsessed modern world, it's easy to be precious and paranoid and to strive for an unattainable level of cleanliness. It is unrealistic to think we can always be clean in the city, and it's stressful to try: it fosters unhealthy feelings of ill will and mistrust towards our fellow city dwellers. All we can do is take fate into our own hands and wash them, frequently, hoping that others have done likewise. Don't bite your nails. And don't go licking things.

Is it clean?

2. How to Conduct Relationships

Am I part of the crowd?

So Many People

'We are fond of the crowd and crush, because we are human beings and like to live in groups.'
(LE CORBUSIER, *THE CITY OF TO-MORROW AND ITS PLANNING*)

In his 1929 vision of the utopian city, Le Corbusier identified the needs and functions of his population and segregated the city into work (skyscrapers), travel (underground), recreation (parks) and living (low-rise housing). It is a fanciful and compelling study. Jane Jacobs described it as 'a wonderful mechanical toy'. What I find even more interesting than the fantastical plan itself is Le Corbusier's understanding of our primal behaviour as humans in groups, and how we respond to living in the urban context.

We are animals, still. We are sociable beasts. Today we might be distanced from our animal state by clothing and concrete, but we still have primal urges and responses that govern and shape how we live. In cities, we live in pack-like proximity to a very large number of people. The fortunate majority of us have walls to keep us separated; the sanctuary of private space. Just as we have de-naturalized our animal behaviour, in the city we have constructed a very unnatural habitat in which to live together. Learning how to manage our relationship with this 'crowd and crush', as Le Corbusier describes it, is crucial to managing our physical and emotional well-being in the city.

Chapter One focused on forming a relationship between yourself and the city. In this chapter, we deal with the relationships between city dwellers. We look at the uncomfortable sensation of being so near to, and yet so far from, thousands of other bodies and souls. We unpick the strange vitality and importance of casual acquaintances. We dig into whether the notion of neighbourhood is a sugar-coated fantasy, and ask if communities are all they're cracked up to be. We consider what is public and what is private. We ask basic questions: how do you meet people in a city? How and when do you talk to strangers? We address the challenge of making friends and maintaining friendships. And we grasp the thorny issue of finding love in the city, how to date and how to keep love alive. Finally, we delve into the most important relationship of all: the one you have with yourself. Mastering the art of being alone and content in a crowd is one of the most useful keys to unlocking a happy urban existence.

For as long as humans have existed, we have chosen to live in close proximity to one another to have a better chance of survival. The city is a complex development of this truth. Rather than hunting for food and keeping the fire going, now the city facilitates opportunities of doing business with each other and those further afield. The streets are paved with gold. The future economic output of a country rests more on its cities than its villages.

The potential of people, together, is more than just economic: happiness and quality of life are important parts of the matrix, too. We live together and work together; the more we can improve our relationships, the better chance we have at being a happier and healthier city as a whole.

The Awkwardness of Proximity, Observation and Surveillance

I'm sure we have all heard strangers having sex on the other side of a wall, floor or ceiling. It's a peculiarly visceral experience. I don't mean so much that it awakens the inner pervert in us; rather that it serves to remind us that we are animals living very close to one another. And, although we may be visibly separated from one another, we are often conducting our animal behaviour with barely an inch of plaster separating us from total strangers. One of the danker bedrooms I've lived in had a woefully thin wall, the other side of the neighbour's bathroom through which sound and even smell travelled. It's strange to learn about someone's bowel movements before you know their name. Such is city life.

Most of us live in twentieth- or twenty-first-century buildings that were built using cheap materials, with the minimum of insulation and soundproofing requirements. The footsteps, muffled voices and plumbing sounds of our next-door, upstairs or downstairs neighbours is the white noise of our indoor urban lives. I've wrestled with the discomfort of hearing so much and knowing so little, partly due to my imagination (and my incurable nosiness), which runs wild as I lie in bed wondering about the lives of the people on the other side of the wall. You can smell their cooking, hear what programmes they are watching, catch the odd raised voice; you can hear them playing music in the early hours, getting ready in the morning and closing the door behind them as they step out and begin their public day. This access to others' private lives makes me feel uncomfortable because, just as I can smell, hear and wonder, so too must they be wondering about me.

Finding peace with this low but intimate level of contact is an exercise in diplomacy and tolerance. Knocking on neighbours' doors to introduce yourself might seem friendly, but I'd recommend holding off for a more casual encounter that doesn't involve crossing a threshold into either of your private spaces. What happens next is entirely down to the characters at play. I know people who have developed lifelong friendships with their neighbours. I also know people who have been forced to move on due to tricky and stubborn neighbours. It's the roll of the dice. On the subject of tolerance, though, it's important not to cast yourself as the difficult one. I'm sure many of us have been in apartment blocks with a neighbour who makes it his or her business to find fault and inconvenience in everything. Living in a building with someone who habitually leaves scratchy messages full of capital-lettered words and exclamation marks is no fun. If you have a problem with someone else's behaviour (or if they have a problem with yours), it's better to sort things out in person than let the issue fester. Making these relationships respectful, grown-up, tolerant and human works best for everyone.

Hearing (and occasionally smelling) your neighbours' habits is one thing. Seeing them is something different. Recently I lived in a tiny Dickensian garret flat on a historic market street in central London. From my dormer windows I could see clearly into the

Is there anybody there?

residential building on the opposite side of the street. At the time I smoked, and so was routinely at the window. My casual voyeurism was not sinister and I never found myself in a *Rear Window* situation, thank goodness. But I was fascinated by the entirely mundane habits of other people's lives (NB these were living rooms, not bedrooms). There was the suited city gent who would come home from work every day and walk around in his boxer shorts for the rest of the evening; the girl whose kitchen was more like a launderette because she ironed constantly; the young couple who lay on their sofa night after night watching, or working from, their own separate screens; the mysteriously dingy room that changed hands monthly, and always housed night owls. The most fascinating thing of all was that the curtains or blinds in any of these windows were so rarely, if ever, drawn. The life on show was unremarkable, and charming for it. It's life-affirming to realize that so many of your neighbours are just like you. I wondered if everyone unconsciously felt that they had nothing to hide, so why hide their lives from the city with curtains? Has social media trickled into our physical lives to the extent that we are now happy to share a lot more than a newspaper article we've enjoyed? For sure, our boundaries between what's public and private have definitely slackened, and I realized on considering this that I too had kept my living room curtains open ever since moving in. I eventually gave up smoking, and my time at the window became less frequent. I still never closed my curtains, though, and occasionally wondered if anyone was looking in and watching me eat yet another takeaway.

Surveillance is a weighty issue these days. Living in a city, it's impossible not to be overlooked – if not by eyes across the street, then certainly by CCTV, and if not by CCTV then apparently by the many websites and platforms we've given personal details to. In our post-Snowden era we are beginning to understand the extent to which we have relinquished our privacy, and the potential impact of this on our lives. It feels uneasy and uncannily Orwellian. But watching each other in the city can still be innocent. Think of it like a dialled-down version of the Neighbourhood Watch curtain-twitchers, whereby you're just aware of who is around you and what they are doing. You don't have to take up smoking like a teenager and hang out of your windows like I did. Just keep your eyes open. It's about being plugged in and observant rather than nosey or gossipy.

The Small Acquaintances

We've established, then, that cities are about people more than buildings. When we think of the people we cross paths with, it's easy to think of two camps: those we know and those we don't. The first camp consists of our close network: our family, friends, friends of friends, colleagues, neighbours and maybe our hairdresser. The other is everyone else. Except there is a tranche of people missing from this binary outlook: the acquaintances we see daily, weekly and even monthly as part of our routines. These people work at shops we frequent. They serve us coffee and drinks and food in our favourite local pubs or restaurants. They run the fruit stall you walk past every day on your way to work. You have a presence in each other's lives. They know your face and your habits, although they may not know your name.

These relationships are far more important to the fabric of the city and your life within it than you might think. Jane Jacobs writes beautifully and succinctly on this matter: 'Cities are full of people with whom . . . a certain degree of contact is useful or enjoyable; but you do not want them in your hair. And they do not want you in theirs either.' It is this unspoken, mutual recognition that is key to fostering these relationships. Much as my mother would like it otherwise, you simply cannot invest in every person with whom you come into contact on a daily basis in the city. It is unrealistic, however much emotional energy you may be bursting with. The man who serves you coffee might get to know your name, your order and throw you the odd pleasantry; generally speaking, this is a sufficient scaffold for a relationship that matters in its own right. It is familiar and it is friendly without needing to step into the category of friendship. It is civic civility.

Why do these relationships matter? Because they root us. These small acquaintances humanize the formality of day-to-day urban living. Imagine replacing your coffee stop with a vending machine, your dry cleaner with a robot and your teenage till boy with a cranky self-checkout station always telling you there's an unexpected item in the bagging area. Your daily rituals would become mechanized and devoid of human contact. There would be no one to lift your dulled spirits with a smile. Trite as that sounds, we are bound by codes of behaviour when surrounded by other people that encourage us to make an effort. Be polite and smile back. These small encounters level us, and can be humbling and uplifting in equal measure.

They matter for another reason too, though, and that is security. There is a casual trust implicit in our relationships with people who see us every day. When I drop into conversation that I will be away for two weeks the fruit-stall lady outside my apartment will, unprompted, offer to keep an eye out. I can leave my keys with the dry cleaner for someone else to pick up, without any suspicion. I'm sure we are all familiar with that gratifying feeling of having our coffee or drink order given to us before we've asked. It means recognition, which in turn makes us feel that we belong.

What Is a Good Neighbourhood?

A neighbourhood is a sense of community rooted to a particular place. The butcher, the baker, the candlestick maker. The animal pack, even. Everyone has a place and plays a part, fitting together like a jigsaw. The neighbourhood is a social construct that enables people to live, work and play together in close quarters with a feeling of engagement and security beyond their existence as individuals.

'It has a great neighbourhood feeling' is a phrase we often hear when someone talks up the area they live in. What they tend to be implying is that it has a sense of scale and community that is manageable, more village-like than urban. The most attractive neighbourhoods aren't just the ones with tidy streets and park benches; they're the ones where there's a palpable sense of an open, rather than closed, community. Being a good neighbour is not about watching from behind your curtains and reporting any suspected misdemeanour to the police – it's about inhabiting your neighbourhood beyond the curtains, bringing life to your streets with open arms, not closed minds.

Copenhagen is often held up as a prime example of urban quality of life. People remark that the entire city feels like one big neighbourhood. As part of a project my former employer, the design studio Studioilse, undertook recently, we hosted a small salon dinner, inviting a group of the city's leading thinkers to come and share their thoughts on healthy neighbourhoods. We invited a good cross-section of people to make for a balanced response, which meant that architects and urban planners sat alongside young entrepreneurs and start-ups, graduates, craftsmen and manufacturers, retailers, chefs, creatives and bureaucrats. We handed an envelope out to each person with the question 'What makes a healthy neighbourhood?' on the front and, over the course of the evening, asked them to write an answer on the card inside.

Answers varied enormously. 'A neighbourhood is a collection of stories – the stories of the people that live there and have lived there, the stories of the buildings and the city, which are told through materiality, wear and change. What makes a neighbourhood good is a mixture of fond and well-known stories. New, exciting and foreign stories, so that the anthology is always a mixture of memories and hopes.' This response has stayed with me. It captures beautifully the elasticity of time and change and the relationship between place and people. ('The smell of meatballs' was an unexpected response but equally poetic, to my mind.)

Consensus was reached on the need for 'a mix' and for tolerance; neighbourhoods should be inclusive, not exclusive. Jan Gehl, a very great Dane indeed and arguably one of the world's greatest urbanists, said that to make a good neighbourhood, you must burn down the kindergarten. He explained this with an anecdote about a suburb of Copenhagen where the kindergarten burned down (at night, thankfully) and, facing the challenge of what to do, the previously disparate local population instantly came together into a community. Gehl's point was that 'a common problem' is vital in forming a good neighbourhood.

How can you, the individual, make your presence felt as part of the neighbourhood? Once again, it's about being open, not closed. Be visible. Don't skulk. You don't have to call or chair community gatherings, but make use of community services and local businesses wherever possible. Be aware of the key players in your area's politics (both official and unofficial). If your neighbourhood should happen to come up against any problem that requires involvement from higher up the city ladder, a loud, collective community voice is more likely to be heard and answered than a confused babble of lone voices. This point was made with extraordinary clarity by Ione Wells, a twenty-year-old student who was sexually assaulted one night in London close to her own front door. She wrote a defiant open letter to her attacker that led to a campaign against victim blaming, and it stunned the nation with its candour. She wrote that she was a daughter, a friend, a girlfriend, a pupil, a neighbour and an employee who served everyone down the road coffee in the cafe under the railway arch: 'All the people who form those relations to me make up my community and you assaulted every single one of them.'

How and When Do You Talk to Strangers?

'"What would you do as Mayor?"
"Tell everyone to take the day off, sit in the sun and just
talk to each other. There's not much of that spirit in
London now."'

(DAVID HASSELHOFF, 'MY LONDON', *EVENING STANDARD*)

The American actor David Hasselhoff (or Mitch from *Baywatch*, as many might know him) may not seem an obvious source of insightful commentary on urban life, but his point is valid. We talk less to each other now, and the city is a sadder place because of it. One of the oddest realities of living in a city is being surrounded by so many people with whom you never interact. The level of contact we have with our hypothetical neighbours varies across city and culture. In London, people tend to avoid meeting the eyes of their fellow commuters; in warmer countries, sometimes the people seem warmer too. Conversations among strangers are more common in Spain, France, Italy and Greece than they are in the UK, Sweden or Germany; cold and warm climates certainly have an impact on our personalities. A journey on public transport in your city should give you a fairly accurate sense of the local custom regarding stranger engagement.

The fact is, however, that we are social beings, regardless of culture – and research increasingly shows that loneliness, silence and lack of human contact have severe repercussions on our health and well-being. Recent research by the charity Age UK revealed the deeply troubling fact that a million elderly people in Britain had not spoken to a single person in the past month. Although the idea of being isolated and alone in later life is harrowing, the state of being lonely and silent around one another is a social epidemic from which we are all suffering. Fortunately there are an increasing number of initiatives, big and small, geared to shake us out of this silent sickness.

It's a paradox of modern times that the more we engage with social media in our virtual lives, the more antisocial we become in reality. I firmly believe that the tide is beginning to turn, and we are reawakening to the joy of analogue human contact. The great tech success stories that feel contemporary and relevant today are the ones that reduce friction in our lives and bring us together as people, not the ones that create artificial networks or barriers to hide behind. The sharing economy brought to life by the likes of Airbnb, Carshare and BorrowMyDoggie might sound radical at first; but isn't it really just a reframing of that old value of neighbourliness, aided by technology? Against this backdrop of social change, the time is ripe to step out from the Twittersphere and engage with people rather than their profiles. It seems ridiculous that so many of us are happy to engage in virtual conversations with strangers, yet remain silent in a group of real people.

What does it take to break the impasse? Needlework, according to a close friend of mine. She does embroidery, and recently started taking it with her on public transport. She is surprised by the number of strangers who ask her about it. I wonder if they are curious that someone under the age of eighty is doing needlework in public, but she is convinced it's because (for want of a better expression) she is happy to pursue her hobby in public. Putting something out there gets something back. Another friend designs eyewear, and has no qualms in asking strangers about their glasses. She talks of the enjoyment people have in discussing them. It's a safe subject for strangers to talk about because it is visible they have something in common and when my friend remarks on someone else's glasses, she is implicitly complimenting them. A more widespread observation in this vein is that many of us are more than willing to engage with strangers via their dogs.

Signifiers and shared interests are an easy way to break the ice with strangers, and happily, it feels like we are all getting a bit braver. You don't have to take up needlework or get a dog to engage with strangers, though. More often it's about being aware, being alert and taking responsibility for situations. If you find someone lost, ask them if they need help. If you see or sense that someone is in distress, don't leave it up to someone else to step up – chances are, a hundred others have had the same response before you. Be the rock against the flood. I'm sure we've all seen someone else break that flow of apathy and take control of a situation in a way that's made us regret not responding sooner ourselves.

In extreme circumstances, where incident tips quickly into crisis, the invisible boundaries between strangers can vanish instantly. Witnessing an accident is a common example of this phenomenon; there's nothing like an act of civic heroism or horror to unite strangers. Thanks to smartphones, the rise of citizen journalism means these acts are being captured and disseminated far more widely today. Footage emerged recently in London of a busload of passengers and pedestrians rocking their bus off the trapped body of a cyclist who'd been run over. Caught on camera, the footage spread around social and mainstream media. That these moments of citizen communion are celebrated is vital, even (maybe especially) in the wake of a horrific incident. They force us to think about how we would respond, which in turn prepares us, should we ever find ourselves in a similar situation.

The city becomes a less intimidating place if we try to think of one another as citizens instead of strangers. Have awareness and respect for your fellow citizens. Next time someone sneezes in your vicinity, say 'bless you', and I guarantee they will smile and say thank you.

Friendships Old and New

If talking to strangers in the city seems difficult, you might expect meeting people and making friends in an urban environment to be a Herculean task. In fact, it's far easier. Cities, by virtue of population size and opportunities for crossing paths, are extremely fertile territory for making friends, and having friends in the city is vital. They are companions for sharing the agony and the ecstasy, drowning out the sorrows and soaring through the highs. They hold your hand and open your eyes. They make you mad and keep you sane. They test and stretch the limits of your emotional portfolio. They are a lifeline.

Different people bring out different elements of our personalities, and you don't have to bring all your friends together and make them friends with each other too – compartmentalizing friends and friend groups is a perfectly healthy approach. And, despite what some people say, you are never too old to make new friends. If people are continually fascinating, then friendships between them are even more compelling.

Advice on how to make friends can be reduced to the following two rules, unchanged since your schooldays: opt in, and be yourself. Do things. Join things. Sign up and share parts of your life with others. If you hide yourself and your feelings behind too many projections or personas, you won't attract playmates that connect with who you genuinely are; they can only connect to the person you put out there. Being yourself and holding on to yourself is a tricky thing to master at any stage in life, wherever you are. And it's trickier still with the many-layered crush of the city to navigate at the same time. But the goal of building relationships with integrity is one worth striving for.

Today, nobody really knows nobody in a city. When I was working at *Monocle* magazine and travelling constantly as part of my job, it amazed me that, from Sarajevo to Tbilisi to Okinawa, all it took was just one family member or friend to connect me to someone they knew who would happily meet me and introduce me to their lives. These were not friendships per se, but it struck me that were I to uproot myself to any of these distant cities, making friends might not be so difficult after all. Our networks are extensive today, aided by the internet, social media and the increasingly transitory, nomadic lives we all live. Meeting people with whom we might have something in common, almost anywhere in the world, has never been easier. And for friends old and new, whether at home or out on the tiles, the city is a veritable playground of experiences waiting to happen.

There are things we can do to feed this social network. Bring people together you think might get along or be able to help each other in some way. Connecting people socially and professionally is a generous habit that inspires goodwill. It is contagious, and it keeps our networks fluid and active. Arrange a dinner and suggest your friends bring someone else along.

What shall we do?

Cultivating friendships is crucial, but it's worth adding a note of caution about giving away all of yourself to too many people too quickly. It's vital we leave time and space for ourselves (more on this shortly). I'm sure many of us have experienced being drawn into an intense friendship with someone before realizing that, for one reason or another, it just isn't going to be a good fit. It's far more difficult to end a friendship than to begin one. Be aware, rather than wary.

I'm Afraid I'm Busy

So it's a given that friendships are vital to a fulfilled urban existence. Why is it, then, that so many of us find it difficult to make plans with our friends – then resent the plans that we do make, and even feel relieved if the plans fall through? It's no mark of how much we (dis)like the friends in question. When the plans don't fall through, we most likely have a wonderful time and all previous thoughts of resentment either vanish or twinge us with guilt.

These perplexing feelings are not an indication that we are in fact solitary creatures. I used to worry that I was inherently antisocial because the idea of going out seemed so unappealing. The truth of the matter is that daily city life is exhausting, and making plans with friends can often feel like 'just one more thing' – an optional extra on top of all our daily obligations.

It is important to think about the friends that you have and what they bring out in you. Discussing this fact with a range of people revealed that we all have the odd friend we value and love but somehow dread seeing. This is because they require more emotional investment and time than they put in. An innocent drink after work can leave you stumbling home after midnight, rinsed of body and mind. It might not sound like a healthy way of conducting a friendship, but we all go through ebbs and flows in life that require different levels of attention and support from our friends. We should remember the times when others have been there for us the next time we feel a yearning to cancel something due to a work crisis.

General belief has it that, as we settle over time, slow down, forge relationships and maybe have children, our social lives take a back seat. I used to look forward to weeks and gloriously empty weekends in which to be my own boss and do exactly as I wished. In fact, the older I become, the stronger the tug towards genuine friendship feels – by which I don't mean the FOMO described in the previous chapter. It's more the spontaneous phone call, the lunchtime glass of wine, the planned Sunday lunch. Perhaps it's the softening of the heart that comes with age. But far from receding into my armchair and slippers with dignity, I feel more inclined than ever to say yes, not no, and I feel happy and vitalized as a result. This is not to say I don't look at my diary at the start of a week or month and feel panicked that there is far too much scrawled on every day and night already. It is a truth, however, that city life is better the more effort you make and the more connected you are to your real social network. Friendships require feeding to grow.

Put Down Your Phone and Fall in Love

Given that the city is so densely populated, it stands to reason it must be easy to find the perfect match, right? Well, this is true to a point.

We are surrounded by opportunities to meet the man/woman of our dreams as we come into contact with thousands of strangers. We've heard the songs, seen the films, read the books – maybe we even have a friend who locked eyes with their future partner across a crowded train/bar/club, and that was that. The timeless fairytale of love at first sight is still perpetuated.

There is such a thing as too much choice, though, and the proliferation of dating sites and apps we currently live with has exploded the process of meeting potential partners into something altogether more virtual and warped. Rather than making it easier to meet people, it can make us feel even more isolated. Tinder, Grindr, Match.com and a thousand others are enabling tools, no doubt. But on the flipside, their proliferation might also be indicative of the diminishing awareness we have of each other in public space nowadays, given how permanently buried we are in our smartphones. A face-to-face, love-at-first-sight encounter seems impossible. It's a cruel paradox that the very tools designed to bring us together are creating a greater distance between us than ever.

I sound like my grandmother, but it horrifies me to read reports that teenagers will send naked pictures of themselves to their classmates but not speak to each other in person. One can only hope this is a cruel combination of puberty and technology that will iron itself out with time. Yet there are parallels to be drawn with today's adults and their approach to dating. We invest time in crafting the perfect online avatars of ourselves for dating sites in the belief that they will make the hunt easier – that the market is more open, more honest, and that there's not enough time these days to hope you'll bump into Mr or Ms Right in a bar. We create personas, designing what we imagine to be the best versions of ourselves; the pressure to live up to these can be extreme. The giddy high of a 'mutual like' is routinely followed by crashing disappointment when someone who sounded perfect seemingly drops off the face of the earth. My grandmother would have said that this is not a natural pattern of behaviour. I would have replied that online matchmaking works for today's society, and there are countless heartwarming tales and examples to prove it. It is an integral part of how people meet today, and so long as there is the internet, it is impossible to imagine life without internet dating.

But internet dating is not the whole picture. We need to reclaim the city as a net for potential partners in its own right. We all need to work on being better citizens, being more aware of each other and more responsible for each other. This awareness will encourage us to better connect in the physical world, without the need of a helping hand from the virtual one. It seems mad to spend so much time disengaged from the people around you and then to complain that you never meet anyone.

Meeting someone in the city is tougher than it might seem on paper, there's no doubt. It's not about rules as much as guidelines, but it makes sense to be open and take opportunities that arise. Ask to be set up by people you know, and keep your eyes and ears open for others in return. Talk to people that you encounter and feel attracted to. Get involved in activities that you feel might bring you into contact with other like-minded folk. The internet has given rise to all manner of niche groups dedicated to bringing people together for friendship and romance, from singles curry-cooking classes to dance lessons, pottery and book clubs. Sign up for something with a friend. And if you meet someone you find interesting, be brave and initiate the

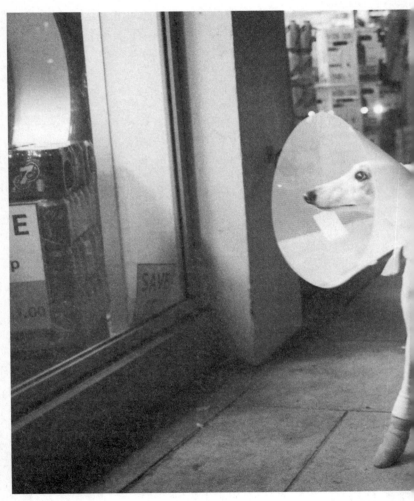

Take me home?

offer of a date. It takes two to tango, but it always takes one person to ask another to dance. Don't sit and wait.

Once you've found someone, how do you negotiate the city and your life in it with a potential partner? One of the best feelings in the world is seeing your city through the eyes of a loved one, and showing them your world in return. Cities have never felt more exciting, invigorating and filled with opportunity than when you are falling in love. Every moment and experience feels ripe for a song and a memory. The most insignificant things are pregnant with emotion and meaning. It is a time to be indulged in as one of life's great joys. Just be mindful not to lose your grip on reality and the real person in front of you; fall in love with the person, not the romance of being in love.

The city is the perfect stage on which to play out the beginnings of your relationship, but it can throw up its own obstacles. 'Take time and make time,' someone wise advised me when I was panicking that my exciting new flame was going to burn out before it had begun. We were incapable of finding dates at regular intervals that suited us – it was starting to look as if being busy meant being single too. But I was determined that the crowded schedule I'd once used as an excuse not to be in a relationship should not now jeopardize my chances of making a relationship work. So I invited him into my busy-ness, and soon realized two things. Firstly, that it was fine (and fun) to include him. Secondly, that I wasn't really as busy as I'd always thought – it was a hangover state of mind from my days of single self-protection. Nobody is too busy to fall in love.

Being in a relationship in the city can slow you down; as it develops, it forces you to consider the well-being of someone other than yourself. It can help you find calm. It can provide you with a perfect coping mechanism, a crutch, a shoulder, someone with whom to share the highs and lows. Don't shut yourselves away, though – you can continue important parts of your lives independently, together. The balance of strength and vulnerability you need to strike in a romantic relationship is also an important part of the relationship you have with your city – if you are good at one, chances are the other will work well too. A core part of this is about learning when to be hard and when to be soft, something I'll expand on in the next chapter.

All relationships require work, constantly. The city is filled with distractions and it is easy to be sidetracked from facing up to any difficulties you may be having in your relationship behind closed doors. The idea of being single again in the city, having been in a relationship for a while, can feel terrifying to the point where many people decide to put up with a miserable relationship instead. Sometimes it's easier to be extremely busy for a year than admit the fact that your relationship isn't working and needs addressing. But suddenly a year is a decade, and it can quickly become a lifetime. Don't hide behind city life as an excuse. Don't let the city become the third person in your relationship that ends up ruining it. Let it be the backdrop, not the foreground.

How to Be Alone

The most important relationship you must nurture in the city is the one you have with yourself. It is fundamental to your mental, physical, social and emotional well-being. If you don't work at finding peace with yourself, then it will be extremely difficult to form relationships with others. Thankfully we live in a time where opportunities to nurture one's own emotional development are everywhere, and continually expanding.

As the world around us develops rapidly, it is more important than ever that we know ourselves. It is important that we recognize our capabilities and limits, our strengths and weaknesses. We must find ways to be at peace with ourselves before we find ways to be at peace with others.

We all know that you can feel lonely in a crowd – and that there is a difference between being alone and being lonely. Sara Maitland's fascinating exploration of the boundaries of solitude and loneliness is the subject of a previous book in the same series as this one – *How to Be Alone*. In it, she traces the subtle difference between feeling lonely and being alone. Feeling lonely suggests you have a yearning to be with others; being alone suggests contentment in your solitude. I have repeatedly stated that we are social animals by virtue of being human, but our lives cry out for a degree of alone time too. It is crucial to spend time by yourself. You need time and space to confront yourself, to stay sane, to learn about yourself and to like yourself. In most cities, where the ratio of people to space technically leaves each of us with less than a square metre of personal space, we all need to work hard to create space around us, inside and outside our heads. This can be achieved in all manner of ways, from learning how to regulate your breathing to practising meditation to going to the cinema, a gallery or for a meal by yourself. One of my favourite things is taking a walk after dark, late at night when the streets are empty and you feel a different side of your familiar city entirely.

How Technology Is Changing Our City Experience

What did we do before Google Maps and Citymapper? In fact, what did we do before smartphones, before we had the internet in our pockets, before we had cameras on our phones, before we even had mobile phones? Today we can time our bus arrival to the minute, map our quickest route to anywhere, have a taxi pick us up in moments whenever we want without exchanging cash, find a spare room or even a flat, hunt for flatmates of any age, gender, ethnicity, sexuality. We can order most foods to come to our door. We can find someone within a distance of metres who might be interested in having sex. We can take photos and instantly send them to the world for rating and commenting. We can be informed of any news from anywhere, almost as soon as it happens.

Technology has transformed how we live in the city and it's diffi-cult to get a grip on how this might evolve, given the sheer speed of developments in the last decade or even year. The city comes to us now. Serendipity is rarer than ever. Just as we have eliminated so many inconveniences from our urban lives, so too have we written out the potential for much magic and surprise. Many will argue that cities have never been easier to live in and that our cleverer technology is the reason for this. There can be no doubt that technology is giving us an urban experience with fewer bumps in it. But is this a good thing?

In writing this book I was determined to shed the scales of urban fatigue from my eyes, to properly watch and assess – not only to rely on received wisdom or past experiences, but to test my beliefs about city life in real time. If I had to identify the most important thing I've learnt from this process, it would be that we now rely on

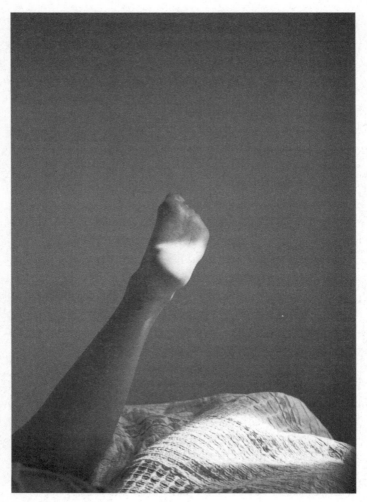

Am I alone or lonely?

technology to an extent I'd considered but never appreciated fully. We have devolved so much responsibility for our urban experience to our phones. The majority of us are plugged in and listening to or watching something on our phones – in isolation, in couples, in groups, on the move, in restaurants, in idle moments and active moments. A study in 2013 by Nielson in the US revealed that Americans spend on average 70 per cent of their time awake in front of digital media. We are living vicariously through our pocket devices. Our screens have become shields from real life.

My intention has been to offer ideas and suggestions – to open your eyes to the importance of being human in the city, of feeling connected and of slowing down. I believe that feeling like a human, behaving like a human, responding like a human to others and to your surrounding environment is the key to living a fulfilled life in the city. Once I felt that the city was the enemy, encouraging us to behave in an inhuman way; today, I see technology as a significant obstacle to developing healthy relationships with our environment and with each other. In the wake of our ever-developing, embedded technological advances, let's not forget how to be human. After the initial horror, leaving your phone at home can sometimes be a wonderful thing.

3. How to Be Hard and Soft

Can we slow down?

What Is a Work/Life Balance?

That you are reading this book tells me it's likely you have considered the value of a meaningful job. It is an important marker of our continued development that an increasing number of us are no longer willing to sign off our working hours to something we don't believe in. Something we don't love, even. The blue- and white-collar days of yore fostered a sense of duty and endurance in our forebears. Working to live, not living to work, was the norm. For a few decades of transition we were mildly scorned by certain puritanical voices for being soft and indulgent, striving to find work that made us happy beyond keeping us dry and fed. Today, though, you need only cast your eye over the bestseller lists to see books that promote the value of taking control of your professional life. Matthew Crawford's books, in particular *The Case for Working with Your Hands: Or Why Office Work is Bad for Us and Fixing Things Feels Good*, have spawned a growing movement of people determined not to get stuck behind a desk. Apprenticeship schemes are being promoted heavily by governments and industries across the developed world as an important way of boosting employment. More than this, they are a crucial way of transferring knowledge by learning on the job, retaining key skills at a local or national level, fostering professions and professionalism.

When I graduated (shortly after the millennium) there was still a clear divide between those who wanted to make a lot of money quickly at the expense of their happiness, and those who were happier to head out into the unknown and find a job that chimed with their interests and values, even if it meant a struggle. We all moved to London, and our experience of the city was intertwined inextricably with the choices we'd made. Though a gross simplification, it's fairly accurate to say the lawyers, management consultants and bankers spent weekdays and weeknights out of contact and spent weekends making up for lost time in a hedonistic haze. The rest of us (entrepreneurs, charity workers, architects, journalists/artists/actors, to name a few) explored the city through our work. Weeknights were like weekends, more often than they should have been. It's not to say that work wasn't taken seriously – more that it was enjoyed as part of life, as part of getting to know the city, as a party. Five years later, everyone wondered if they'd made the right decision after all. We were split into two camps, and we envied each other's green grass. There were those who could afford to dine out whenever and holiday wherever, but felt like life with money was not necessarily life with meaning, and life in general was passing them by. And there were those who were left with £10 to see them through the last week of every month, who wondered if city living was just too expensive for anyone who worked in a creative field.

Since then, life has changed considerably for all involved. The recession was an awakening. Value and values were reassessed, some forcibly, some on their own terms; articles about macro-banker-turned-micro-brewer filled newspaper supplements at the weekends. It might still be too soon to talk sensibly about the generational fallout of the global financial crisis, but as things reshuffle into some semblance of near-stability, it seems that the 50/50 'us and them' divide between cash-no-morals and morals-no-cash has dissolved. The search for meaningful work is becoming ever more widespread and mainstream. Chasing a career for status or money in place of fulfilment, and at the expense of happiness or values, seems archaic today.

Curious as to whether other people shared my thoughts, I asked my friends a few questions. One was 'do you feel you have a work/life balance?' I was careful to include a cross-section of age, job and wealth. I was surprised that every single person remarked on the fact work/life balance doesn't really apply to them nowadays because their job is their life, and vice versa. You could interpret this as a miserable or triumphant leap forward for the world of work. Everyone in some way commented on the mobility of the office: that desk jobs are slowly dying, as technology allows us to check our emails in the middle of dinner or in the middle of the night. Work comes with us everywhere. Of course, it's impossible to maintain a work/life balance when we are all so addicted to our mobile offices. The upside of this fairly dystopian slide is that our tolerance levels for the kind of work we do have been positively affected too. If we are to be permanently tethered to our work, then we are far more willing to hunt down, fight for and hold on to a job that matters to us and that makes us happy.

Understanding the position of work in your life is one of the core tenets of The School of Life – coming to terms with it, getting control over it, finding meaning in it. Mastering a work/life balance in the city is hard, because you have to fight not to get stuck in the hamster wheel. But in other ways, it's easier than it might be elsewhere. A wealth of people brings a wealth of opportunity. Seeking opportunity is the challenge. Having the confidence and courage to seize it and run with it is something that requires strength. I believe we have entered a new age where collaboration, not competition, is our modus operandi. Have faith: finding meaningful work with other people, through other people and for other people has never been easier. This chapter is about when to be hard and when to be soft in the city – which means understanding when to show your steel and when to reveal your vulnerability. It's about work, rest and play, and how to achieve some semblance of balance in each. The greatest foundation you can have for this is a job that you enjoy, one that you are happy to embrace and embed into your life.

Dealing with Stress and Avoiding Ruts

Stress is the great epidemic of our times. We all suffer constantly from it, to varying degrees. We blame it for things we can't easily explain. It makes us ill. It keeps us awake. It makes us unhappy. It makes us drink too much. It stops us being sociable. It stops us being nice. And in the end, we are told, it even kills us. Cities are inherently stressful because stress is contagious, from one area of our lives to another and even from person to person. Stress about work becomes stress about money, which becomes stress about home, which becomes stress about your relationship.

How do you cope? It is unrealistic to think that you can eliminate stress from your life in its entirety. Learning to live with it, to be in control of your stress levels and to channel stress into a more positive energy are easier targets. We all know about the active things we can do such as taking regular exercise, practising meditation and seeking therapy when it all becomes too much to cope with alone.

There are other ways, too. Use the city to its advantages; instead of locking yourself away in a spiralling state of anxiety, use your social networks (by which I mean real, more than virtual). Stress is a feeling of being overwhelmed, of being worried and scared, of feeling incapable, feeling alone. Facing up to things that cause you stress is the most empowering way of beating them. Push yourself out of your comfort zone. Vocalizing your fears and anxieties demystifies them and brings them out of the cavernous, irrational territory of your own head. It stops them from slipping into your subconscious, bedding down, growing and looming. Share them with people who you allow to comfort you. 'Worries shared are worries halved,' my parents have always said, and it's a valuable lesson.

Share your stress with others who have less investment in your emotional well-being, too. Talk about an anxiety to someone at work, or a friend of a friend at dinner. We are better at offering each other advice and solving each other's problems when we aren't clouded by any emotional impact. Showing vulnerability and being able to talk openly about it is not weak; it's strong and attractive. Use these networks to ask for advice, from how to deal with particular situations and circumstances to recommendations for an acupuncturist, personal trainer or therapist. Sharing experiences and helping others is generous and healthy. Just don't become the moaner who constantly asks for advice and never listens to the answer; there's a fine line between attractively vulnerable and irritatingly needy. Try to be aware of the balance in what you give and what you take.

The closer the friendship, the more elastic this can be, but taking too much and not giving enough in return can still cause the closest friendships to snap.

It's not defeatist to accept stress as part of one's life in the city. Understanding its sources and learning how to cope with it is the key to not letting it destroy you. Finding your work stressful does not mean you need to find a new job; the external pressures of work and city living are demanding enough that you shouldn't add to your own stress with constant self-flagellation.

Instead, be on your own side, and take active steps to release the pressure if you feel it's getting too much. Write a list of your anxieties – sometimes all it takes is to commit them to paper to make you aware of how insignificant they might be, or to help you think of ways to reduce them. Often, when you break stress down into its component parts, you can find manageable ways of alleviating it. Plot ideas for solutions, and set yourself realistic targets and goals of how you might achieve them. Know your strengths, and consider what you can achieve alone and what you might need help with. Understand what and who makes you feel happy and strong, and seek these activities and people out. Embed them in your life and routine.

Cities are ripe territory for ruts, too. Because the city is intense we tend to focus on the immediate demands of day-to-day living, and it can be hard to find the extra energy required to break free of them. Ruts – at work, in your living situation, in your relationship – can restrict our thoughts and actions to the point where we feel like we are drowning in a self-perpetuating fug of misery, and we no longer have the imagination or energy to do anything about them. The secret to dealing with ruts is similar to dealing with stress – not surprising, as both problems are symptoms of city life getting the better of you. Try to take yourself out of your comfort zone to understand what the problem is, and think clearly about what you can do about it.

Distancing yourself to achieve an objective outlook on your situation might be as simple as breaking your routine to make familiar, unconscious actions feel significant and conscious again. Try getting up an hour earlier, or going for a walk in the evening instead of watching TV. It's like kick-starting your mind. Once you've established the distance, ask yourself what it is that's unsatisfying about your lot. Write down how you got to this state and what, realistically, you can do to change things in the short term and the long term. Once you have clarity on the bones of the situation, open up about it and elicit the advice and support of others. At work, try talking to your manager about a shift in direction, taking on a new challenge or even moving desks for a change of scenery. At home, consider whether the way you're using your space really suits the way you live. Sometimes rearranging the furniture is all that's needed to reinvigorate your sense of sanctuary. When you're in one, a rut can seem intimidatingly difficult to escape from; but as with so much of life, getting perspective, breaking the situation down and making a written plan of action is an extremely helpful way to move forward.

And moving forward is arguably the greatest way of dealing with most of the difficult symptoms of city life. It allows you to feel in control, and that is empowering. Embrace change. Keep your imagination active. Be courageous, and don't worry about making decisions that turn out differently from how you'd expected. Don't be scared of admitting you've made a mistake, either. As Oscar Wilde said, 'Experience is simply the name men give to their mistakes.'

Being Bored: Good or Bad?

After stress and ruts comes another typically urban ill: boredom. There's still an odd stigma attached to boredom, which too often implies it is the fault of the bored person. 'Only boring people are bored,' is a common refrain that sounds like it came from the Victorian nursery. The suggestion that being bored is bad is fairly nonsensical, in my opinion. Feeling boredom is allowing yourself to disengage. It is putting your conscious on standby for a while and letting your subconscious float to the surface. There's a reason why many of us have our best ideas in the shower; this is a routine moment of disengagement when our autopilot takes over, and we don't have to actively think about what we are doing. Allowing boredom into our lives is similar. Boredom is an important part of human existence, and in the city it is a crucial part of your toolkit for letting off steam and allowing yourself to recalibrate.

The typical criticism of the bored is that they're not able to engage with the stimuli around them, and that they must therefore be deficient. In a city there are so many stimuli – therefore there must be something for anyone, surely, no matter what their character or mood? But cities are overstimulating, and we can only take so much. Being ceaselessly active in body and mind is not necessarily fulfilling; it can be exhausting. Today we are more stimulated than ever by the surge of news, social contact and commercial invasion that hits us from our phones, our computers and the streets beyond. We have less and less control over how and when we plug in or out. Being bored, and allowing boredom as a state of mind to enter your life, is a necessary foil to this. Boredom is our power-saving mode.

Aldous Huxley described boredom as a 'symbol of liberty . . . excessive freedom'. It is a very modern luxury, an indulgence. As with any treat, we musn't overindulge and boredom shouldn't be your default setting – but embracing it as part of your repertoire is healthy, like a form of passive meditation. It allows you to create space to think to yourself. It creates room to breathe and slows you down. It allows for spontaneity and serendipity. It encourages your subconscious to speak to you. It is a transitional state between feeling active and passive, and it's in this state that we can pay better attention to both body and mind.

How can you foster boredom? Try doing nothing by yourself. Make plans to see no one for an hour or two at the weekend. Don't read. Don't sleep. Don't reach for your laptop. Don't busy yourself with chores. Don't actively think about anything. Just exist. Hear things rather than listen for them. See things rather than look at them. Go for a walk with no destination. Let your gut guide you. These voids of time, spent in a vacuous state with only yourself for company, can be surprisingly energizing.

Sometimes It's Fine to Stay in Bed

The common thread through this chapter has been about cutting yourself some slack and letting yourself off the hook. That's not to say you shouldn't have ambitions, or strive for a more fulfilling life; it's more that to achieve this you have to know yourself, recognize your own strengths and allow for your weaknesses. City living is tough. It's an assault on your physical, mental and emotional well-being.

Can I stay here all day?

It requires energy in reserves that even the best-slept, healthiest humans struggle to muster. It is thrilling and exhausting, punishing and pleasurable, and it is fine to be selfish sometimes. More than fine – it is necessary. It is fine to cancel things because you can't face them, so long as you're not letting someone else down horribly. Sometimes when it's pouring with rain and you feel shattered, it's fine just to stay in bed all day. And don't torment yourself about it. Mental and physical exhaustion grind us down over time and make us ill. You're only human if you let guilt creep up on you when you think about all those things you could be doing, but consider how many hours of overtime you've given to work and count them as time justifiably earned in the bed bank.

How to Have Extra-Curricular Interests and Not Become a Bore

Tiring as cities are, it would be foolish to spend *all* your free time in bed. There is a lot to do beyond your front door, and you'd be mad not to make the most of what is on offer. We all know people who rampantly 'do' things: pasta-making classes, reptile taxidermy, merengue dancing, upholstery lessons, an Ikebana course. Taking advantage of the many things a city has to offer is admirable, but collecting experiences in this way can feel strangely soulless.

Successful living in the city is about knowing what to let wash over you, and when to plunge deep. Learning, mastering and practising something extra-curricular is an opportunity to explore depth, not skim across the surface. Do something with the intention of getting good at it. Do it because you genuinely want to do it, not because you feel you should or because it's something to talk about that makes you sound interesting. The city offers the opportunity to find people to share our interests with, to learn from and to impart our own knowledge and experience too. It's an important form of social contact that being in the city enables. It makes us feel connected to others through shared interests.

Even though we generally know what we are good at and what we enjoy doing, finding hobbies we love can be strangely elusive. The biggest obstacle is usually you. When we already feel squeezed for money, time and energy as it is, the idea of introducing another regular activity to our diaries can feel punishing. The truth is, of course, that we can always make time for the things we love doing. A good place to start is to think back to childhood, when many of us were kept occupied at home and at school with activities we perhaps didn't appreciate at the time and couldn't wait to drop. On reflection, did you maybe find singing in the choir satisfying? Were you actually a bit of a natural with a paintbrush, or on the piano? Do you wish you'd kept up with your badminton? From car motorbike mechanics to wooden-spoon whittling, meat-carving to mouth-organ groups, cities offer a plethora of skills to master. Often breaking the barrier and actually enrolling on something is the scariest hurdle. An easy way around this is to pair up with someone you know shares your interests. Having a partner to do things with doesn't just reduce the initial five seconds of terror, but will hopefully ensure you stick it out in times when you might feel inclined to sack it off.

Being in Public

Cities gave birth to the need for delineation between private and public space. Whether temple, forum, baths, theatre, coffee houses or parks, a significant portion of our lives in cities, throughout history, has been conducted in space designated as public. This is partly because most people's living space is too small to accommodate all the functions we need to live a healthy life. We cannot be self-sufficient in cities in the way we can be in a rural habitat. But it is also a way of engineering interaction and engagement – trading, preaching, socializing – which feeds the city's growth on so many levels.

Jan Gehl's seminal book on this topic, *Life Between Buildings*, was published in 1971 and sought to restore the balance of public space in cities given to humans, instead of cars. Through a series of simple yet rigorous studies he was able to illustrate that good public space makes for happier residents, and ultimately a healthier city.

With living spaces shrinking for most of us in cities today, we play out more of our lives in public space than ever. It is important we feel comfortable and not insecure. Ilse Crawford is a great proponent of this, highlighting the importance today of feeling 'at home' in public space. The more time we spend in public space that is municipal, clinical or institutional, designed with the ease of cleaning as a priority rather than the pleasure of use, the less pleasure we will have in it and the more alienated we will feel. It should not be a luxury to feel comfortably ourselves in public space.

Public space carries with it a collective responsibility to be considerate of other people. It's not just a duty, though – it's also an opportunity. We should be engaged and responsive, not just responsible. Seek out public space where you feel comfortable – a park, a food market, a cafe, a local pool or theatre. Try not to think of them as just services for use. Give something back by talking to people who work there, bringing friends and introducing them, or even volunteering if the chance arises. Just as the forum was the heart of ancient Rome, so too are our public spaces the lifeblood of our cities today; the more we enjoy using them, the more alive our cities will feel.

Feeding Your Body and Soul

One of the great pleasures of city living is the opportunity to eat good food regularly. Today you do not have to be in the 1 per cent to dine out. A recent report by a US-based food-industry group, the Food Institute, revealed that 43 per cent of every dollar spent by millennials on food is spent in restaurants, rather than at home. Eating out, at markets, trucks, stalls, cafes or restaurants, is part of our daily urban lives. It's how we conduct our relationships, it's how we meet people, it's how we treat ourselves. Eating together feels like a sacred activity that won't be gnawed into by technology. I think this is why we seem to cherish it more than ever.

In the hard, concrete context of the city, fresh food on show in abundance makes us feel alive. Food markets are more than just places to pick up ingredients. They are bursts of life, smell, colour, noise, interaction. They engage so many of our senses all at once, when much of city life can deaden them or persuade us to numb them just to cope. They are an intense dose of nature in an unnatural environment. They are a beating heart. This is why tourist trails so often feature food markets: they are spots in the city where you feel history, culture, commerce and character together at the same time. A market is the perfect place to read every level of the city you are in.

Street food has a similar power over us. It's a form of alchemy watching vast vats of food come to life, being dished out and then disappearing again. I lived for a period on an old weekday food market street in London. Waking up to the clatter of vans and trucks being unloaded, stalls being set up, greetings and gossip being exchanged, was like waking up in the theatre. On my way to work I'd walk down the lane to the sound of chopping, dicing, frying and the smells of raw ingredients being thrown together under heat. When I was at home during the day, the swell of hungry crowds that would gather at lunchtime turned the narrow street into a seething mass of bodies, melted cheese, empanadas and jerk chicken. By the time I came home at night there was no trace of it, bar the odd dirty pigeon picking its way through a few smeared grease wrappers. The rhythm of the street through its daytime ebb and flow was a thing of immense beauty; it is a street that feeds people. It's primal. It is an ancient rhythm played out in streets in cities throughout history the world over.

Finding favourite places to eat in the city is an important part of establishing your stomping ground, the public places in which you feel at home. The place you go for breakfast at weekends, the cafe you frequent for those lunch breaks when you need something more than a sandwich at your desk, the pub where you meet your school friends, the special-occasion restaurant, the suitable-for-parents restaurant, the can't-be-bothered-to-cook-again cafe, the cake-and-ice-cream charm spot, the place to go when it's raining and you feel wretched and need a hug inside. When you begin to piece it together like this, you can easily fill a small address book of food places that have resonance for you at a particular time or need. It's worth culti- vating the list. Frequent places as often as you try new ones. Introduce others to your world of food, and let yourself be introduced likewise. Anyone who's spent time in a city, left, then returned to their former favourite cafe, restaurant or bar will know that it feels like coming home. These are places that feed more than your body. They feed your soul and your relationship with your city too.

Hedonism and Health

You can always find someone to have a drink with in the city. That's one reason why they are fun, and why they can be so dangerous too. It's easy to fill your diary with plans until suddenly you find you've been out every night and are feeling groggy and liverish. We are screamed at by headlines warning us of the dangers of 'middle-class alcohol abuse' and the destructive power of constant wine-drinking. There's little doubt many of us drink too heavily, too frequently. We talk of alcohol as an aid to block out, to relax, to accelerate and stimu- late, to keep us awake and to help knock us out. Drugs are ubiquitous and barely prompt a raised eyebrow. Left unchecked, these habits can easily become addictions, and from there life can quickly descend into a miserable state of affairs.

It is common to hide behind the city and blame it as a foe in this cycle, pointing at the pressure and the ease with which you can indulge. But here, again, a city can be your friend too. Support groups and networks are everywhere, if you have the inclination and muster the courage to look. If you feel strong enough to ask for help, there will be many people on offer to listen and help you. The stigma once cruelly attached to addiction is thankfully a thing of the past. In his introduction to the brilliant essay 'Species of Spaces' (1974), the French writer and philosopher Georges Perec articulated the difficulty of being human in a mantra for life that I carry in my heart: 'There are spaces today of every kind and every size, for every use and every function. To live is to pass from one space to another, while doing your very best not to bump into yourself.'

Looking after ourselves is something we spend our lives trying to master. Understanding the impact that isolated small decisions and choices can make on our lives is a good start. You do not have to shop only in health-food shops to be healthy. But recognize that you have habits or elements of your diet or routine that might, over time, be damaging, and try from one day to the next to change them. Don't be too ambitious – being puritanical doesn't seem to make people much happier or healthier either. Inside we all know what we could or should (or shouldn't) be doing, drinking or eating so much of. Connecting this big-picture impetus to our day-to-day living is where the work lies.

Wellness and well-being are contemporary terms that are becoming increasingly mainstream. In essence they refer to taking positive steps to ensure we are looking after ourselves physically, mentally and emotionally. Embracing well-being is about joining the dots between mind, body and soul, and nurturing a healthy approach to each. San Francisco is a city where much of the population has embraced this, and the city feels vibrant and healthy as a result. The food culture is extraordinarily rich and diverse, working environments place great importance on the healthy stimulation of employees, exercise is an embedded part of life and there is still room for joy and the odd bottle of Napa Valley wine. For a frequent, literal dose of the well-being world, the US-based website wellandgood.com will keep you up to date with nuggets of news and advice.

Well-being is a philosophy too, though, beyond the food and fitness fads. It might sound unlikely but Antoine de Saint-Exupéry's charming allegory *Le Petit Prince* has done more to bring the value systems at the heart of well-being to life for me than any book with the word 'well-being' on the cover. We'd all do well to live by the message in this quote: 'But the eyes are blind, one must live with the heart.'

4. How to Move and Be Still

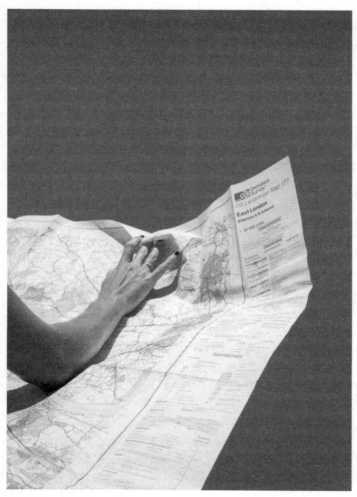

Am I going the right way?

'Life is a journey, not a destination.'
(RALPH WALDO EMERSON)

City life is mobile, not sedentary. We are almost constantly on the move in one way or another, and how we approach this movement is crucial to our well-being. Travelling through the city is how we experience it. We see its best and worst sides. Finding ways to exacerbate the former and minimize the latter is a fundamental part of either loving or feeling defeated by urban life. This chapter is about the many different types of movement in the city. It is about how to cope with the grizzly bits, how to embrace the humdrum and feel euphoric. It's about learning how to switch on your autopilot when you find yourself in the core of an armpit deep underground in the morning. It's about engaging your senses to appreciate the extraordinary in the ordinary. It's about adopting a mindset and, where possible, consciously embracing travel rather than passively enduring it. We spend too much time on the move in the city to not enjoy it.

The Commute

Commuting has a bad reputation. Rush hour, with its tidal surge of tired bodies in tight spaces, can be an overwhelming experience.

We are accustomed to tales of misery: animal behaviour, zombielike reactions, unpleasant sights, sounds and smells, too many people, bad tempers, sweltering underground trains, trudging, slipping, shuffling, pushing and the occasional, accidental yet maddening trip of a shoe. Our commute frames our days; it is the buffer between work and home, private and public. At its worst, travelling en masse to and from work can make us feel less than human. It is when we feel most like cogs in a machine, passively servicing our existence.

Watching commuters in rush hour today can be depressing. Mobile gadgetry might have provided a quiet place of sanctuary to hide in music, pictures and words. But it has also removed us from frequent active engagement with one another. It is a strange twilight state. Eyes down, ears shut. We've all felt that jolt of self-disgust when we've looked up momentarily to realize there is someone in far greater need of our seat standing patiently in front of us.

'How is your commute?' is an early question when talking to city dwellers. Our daily journey is a significant part of our quotidian ritual, and being blessed with a good one has an impact on our sense of happiness with our lot and rightly plays a key part in our decision of where to live and work. A good commute is not only governed by distance. In my working life in London I have lived a five-minute walk from work and was wracked with insomnia. The buffer was too short. I couldn't listen to a song or smoke a cigarette between leaving the office and opening my front door and consequently I carried my working life into my home. I could see my office canteen from my kitchen and bedroom. I have also lived a good hour away from my place of work. And even with tenuous transport connections it was an infinitely happier state of affairs. The route took me by bus through the heart of the city into one of the bigger rail termini and across the city on an underground train to a leafier part of town that was a daily pleasure to walk through. Yes, it was time-consuming and required effort when I was tired, but every day I felt keenly that I was a part of the extraordinary city I lived in.

Commuting is about getting to and from work and it might seem counter-intuitive not to choose the quickest route possible. The fastest is not always the best and not necessarily the most pleasurable. It is surely better to add an extra fifteen minutes if it takes you on a happier journey? A commute can so easily turn into dead time, and as we've explored, the key to living in the city is being alive to most moments. For me this means seeing places that stimulate me. I like crossing the river by foot whenever possible because it feels so intensely London, even if it takes me out of my way. A moment spent looking at the Thames makes me think about London's origins and its rich history. It helps to give me perspective.

Transport networks in most cities are comprehensive enough that you have a choice over how you get from home to work and back again, even if only for part of your journey. Take it into your own hands and try your options. It helps to break the automatic trudge by choosing to do things a little differently on different days of the week. Sometimes it's good to get up early and walk. Go out of your way to visit a good coffee place on your way in. Maybe take a different route in the morning than in the evening. Turn your commute into an experience in and of itself, so that it doesn't become dead time.

Being alert takes practice. You don't have to be blessed with an active imagination to take comfort from the seemingly mundane actions and interactions of daily life that unfold in front of you.

Watch rather than see. Listen to conversations instead of drowning them out with your music. The next time you travel around your city, consider the lives behind the faces you sit opposite or next to. Think of the history in some of the buildings or streets you pass through. It's humbling to consider that you are but one life among many that have trod these paths, past and present. Feel the significance in that. Plug yourself into your urban environment, not your phone.

A commute can also be the perfect opportunity to digest your thoughts. Finding headspace in the city is tough and our commute is a precious daily chunk that we have to ourselves. It helps to park thoughts, decisions or struggles that require active thinking about and save them for a commute when you can give them focused attention. Whether passive or active, use your commuting time, don't fritter it away flicking through Candy Crush Saga.

Goings-on Beneath the Surface

You can read a lot from your city and any city you might visit by what life feels like below ground. Like sweeping things under the carpet, much of the feeling and energy of a city that might be tidily presented on the surface is more difficult to hide underground. The conflict Paris faces between ethnic communities is keenly felt in its metro. There is a palpable bristle in the air, a spark that might ignite at any moment. By contrast the London underground feels solitary and stagnant, filled with a population routinely dissatisfied by the cost and lack of service in return. Pyongyang's beautifully pink and turquoise pastel mosaic underground is reported to be for show only, which would make it a fantastically elaborate ruse. Travelling by subway in Tokyo is a treat, though it has its own sinister side too. That travellers queue politely and neatly fold themselves cheek by jowl into the carriages is deeply efficient of course, but I'm always reminded of that moment in *The Matrix* when Keanu Reeves is told that our earthly experience is just a computer program and humans are in fact being farmed by aliens.

Getting Lost

It's difficult to get lost these days. But providing you're not on your way to an interview, concert or friend in urgent need, I highly recommend it. In the age of technology when we can (usually) be located to within a metre of our whereabouts with a pulsating blue circle on a map, you can find your way anywhere. But then your phone battery dies, and you were trying to take a short cut. You feel a surge of rising dread that there's no one around you to stop and ask, and in your panic you've completely forgotten the name and number of the street where your friend has just moved. *It was all on your phone.*

In the space of a second, you've gone from meandering the streets staring at your location on-screen to being totally reliant on your memory and sense of direction. It's worryingly easy to imagine yourself searching these oddly empty streets forever. Should you just go home, recharge and explain the situation? It feels too defeatist and pathetic to let your own foolishness and your phone dictate your plans to this extent, so you carry on and put yourself in the hands of fate.

Everything feels strangely real now you know you only have your-self to rely on. You turn left and right and left again, feeling a tug in your gut that it must be nearby, given where the pin on the map was. After another fifteen minutes of purposeful searching you find yourself in a leafy residential square that you never knew existed. There's a boules court in the middle of a small avenue of trees, and a nice old pub in the corner. You sit down on a bench and wonder what to do. It's a beautiful autumn day, there's a gentle breeze and just enough warmth in the sun still; though you know it will be one of the last days this year that you can get away with not wearing a jacket. You take a few deep breaths and begin to see the situation for what it really is; it's ridiculous that you haven't written anything down, but how nice it is to have stumbled upon this secret, special little pocket.

The pub landlord lends you a phone charger and you phone your friend to explain what happened and where you are. As luck would have it, she lives just seven minutes away but would like to come and join you there anyway. She's recently moved into the area and has been longing for a game of boules and a few pints. Everything is okay, and you feel thrilled that fate and serendipity have conspired to save you from disaster and reward you with such a good find.

You are never really lost in the city. But feeling lost is a good thing to succumb to occasionally. It encourages us to explore in a way that we don't often allow ourselves time to do, given that we are so busy and time is so precious. And through exploring, we discover things. It's not always a leafy square with a boules court; sometimes it's just an interesting building, a well-tended garden or a plaque telling you your favourite author once lived on this street. The feeling of being lost, once momentary panic has subsided, opens you up to noticing all sorts of things and appreciating them for what they are. It slows you down and makes you feel human.

Being Early and Being Late

Of maybe fifteen people I see fairly regularly, I have just one friend I can count on to always be on time. So much so that it has become characteristic of our meetings that one of us will text the other to say 'on the off-chance you're early again, I'm in this pub on the corner' and it thrills us both that nine times out of ten the other is always hanging around too. I don't know why or how I am always early for everything, but fear of being late governs my movements. It might be a hangover from school, where we were punished severely for being late for anything; or maybe it's just mild neurosis. Whatever, even if I know I am meeting one of my more chronically late friends (there are many), I cannot let myself take their lateness into account when scheduling my own arrival.

It's easy to be sanctimonious about being early. When I think about what it represents, it does annoy me; even if the conscious intention is not there, the unconscious suggestion is that their time is more precious than mine. So I try not to think about it too much. Being late is an urban epidemic. Being early does not imply you are not busy. It is a state of mind, more than anything. It means you are in control, whereas being late (unless there is genuine reason, which of course there often can be) suggests being out of control.

Contrast the feelings you have when you are early with those you have when late. If you are early you might be momentarily annoyed

Am I on time?

that you could have spent a few more minutes doing whatever you were doing before you left. But that soon dissipates into relief, and you realize you have a few minutes to yourself. Here is an opportunity to think, watch and find. It can be a time to digest, to contemplate, to observe, to discover. It's a few moments to slow down, in a life and environment that often move too fast. These moments are precious and the more we build them into our daily lives, the more they help us to feel in control.

Feeling late, on the other hand, is stressful. You rush, you get angry with yourself and others who might be in your way. You feel irrational hatred towards tourists in crowds at the bottom of escalators and train doors that close as you approach them. You feel defeated that things are conspiring against you. You arrive, apologizing, feeling bad, feeling guilty and on the back foot. The urban experience is stressful enough without needing to add to it with too many of these episodes. We can add or subtract a significant amount of difficulty from our daily lives by being the master of our own punctuality. Being late is more often due to a state of mind and habit than circumstance. I believe using our phones for time-keeping has much to answer for, with the inherent distraction they inflict on us. Invest in a watch and take time, both your own and others', seriously.

The Joy of Walking Down a Pavement

Though we might recognize cities from their postcard skylines, it's on the pavements or sidewalks that we really feel them. Pavements are the lifeblood of the human experience in the city, the veins and arteries of the city at human scale.

There are extraordinarily rich layers of life on even the most boring pavement, and learning how to read them is a wonderful experience. Georges Perec described beautifully the 'infra-ordinary' of street observation in his essay 'Species of Spaces'. In it he notes every single detail as he takes it in, pausing to consider why something is the way it is and how it got to be that way. He acknowledges that such close observation of our immediate surroundings takes some work to master, but his point is simple: that we must be present in the moment to appreciate it.

Think of the neon crossing at Shibuya in Tokyo; the piercing light and dark of Manhattan's grid; the manicured evening *passeggiata* in Rome; the electric crush of dusty bodies in São Paulo; the toned roller-bladers of Miami; the clatter and chatter of lunchtime in Beyoğlu, Istanbul. Whether you've been to these cities or not, you can likely conjure up the scene to go with the description because we have all seen pictures or films where such scenarios have played out. When we think about the most vivid streets we've experienced, it's easy to conjure up the epic, the filmic, the representational rather than our own reality. There is validity in these ideas, but they are constructs. The real experience of walking down a pavement in these places is far more visceral, and impossible to capture on film. Try to cultivate your ability to watch, listen and smell in a more attentive way to feel properly connected to your own experience. Walking down a pavement is more than getting from A to B.

Walk down a local street, any street, and take note of your environment, paying attention to one sense at a time. Be curious. For example, I walk down my local street in London and I smell fried chicken. I smell sweat from the man walking in front of me. I smell offal from the butcher. I smell piss under the tunnel. I smell cigarette smoke; I smell weed. I smell air conditioning from the pharmacy mixed with the chemicals of the traffic. I smell heady perfumes, both cheap and expensive, on men and women on their way to work. I hear friends putting a market stall together. One looks like he is teaching the other; is it his first day working on the stall? What does he make of all this? Is it what he thought it would be? I hear a crack addict shrieking at every passer-by for 'some change, luv'. She is high and her voice is frenzied, scared and desperate. I hear schoolchildren loudly and unselfconsciously talking about sex. I hear East End accents and I hear Eastern European ones. I hear snatches of pop and rap through car windows. I hear a toddler being told off by her impatient mother, and I hear babies crying. I hear people talking into their phones everywhere. I see last night's vomit on a street corner. I see a bus stop with more people around it than usual, looking angry. I see one dusty old shop closing down and a new one being painted; the sadness of an ending mixed with the hope of a new start, right next door to each other. I see a broken car window. I see a table of old men eating a fry-up. I see six different dogs being taken for a walk by one man; the dogs seem shy around each other – do dogs get shy when they meet other dogs?

All of this in less than five minutes, on a very unremarkable street. Each sensation feeds the soul, for better or worse, simply by being noticed. As soon as you open yourself up and become conscious and alert to the ordinary, you begin to see the extraordinary in it, and then you find value in so much more of daily life. You do not have to (and possibly shouldn't for your sanity) walk down every pavement noticing everything all the time. But switching yourself on does more than merely open your eyes to your environment; it opens your body and mind too. It allows you to think and feel and be connected to your environment. You are in it, of it and a part of it.

The Soul of the Traditional Taxi

In cities around the world, apps like Uber that offer immediate access to minicabs have transformed how we travel. Many of us don't just rely on these apps – we can't imagine life without them. But they're no friend to the taxi driver of old. Despite the attractive fare difference, we need our traditional taxis on the streets. Call me old-fashioned, but I think minicab apps lack both the human and professional part of the experience that is the intangible soul of taxi travel. The mutual rating systems ensure a level of 'good service', but the process feels eerily robotic. I worry that we are witnessing the decline of a robust profession into an amateur service. There is much to be gained from taking a taxi over the thin layer of convenience or saving of cost that an Uber might offer.

Taxi drivers are more than chauffeurs. They are unofficial custodians of the city and they can be knights in shining armour too, returning phones, wallets, bags and chaperoning single women to their front doors after dark. The knowledge they have of their city is more than the sum of its streets. Taxi drivers don't just know the city like the back of their hand, they have stories to tell about streets you're travelling down, buildings you're passing, tales about the destination you're going to, about famous people they've picked up and things they've witnessed. They are a fount of knowledge and opinion. Ask a taxi driver a question and you never know what you'll get for an answer, but it will doubtless be an honest answer – whereas thanks to the mutual ratings system of Uber, any conversation feels oddly stilted and servile. It's an easy but sadly clinical, transactional experience by comparison.

Be Prepared

I used to envy people who didn't take a bag with them on their journeys around the city. It looks liberating. It suggests a state of at-oneness-with-oneself that you don't need to be accompanied at all times by a clutch of your extraneous possessions. But then a girl I used to work with was struck by a bug on the underground and vomited copiously into the bag she was carrying. The grimness was exacerbated by the fact the poor thing had just bought it at an Yves Saint Laurent sample sale. It was only mildly less humiliating than being sick on her fellow passengers' shoes, and it made me realize that bags have uses beyond simply carrying business cards, ticket stubs and old receipts. If you can carry a phone charger, a notebook, an *A–Z*, some wet wipes, chewing gum, a lighter, lip balm, some nail scissors and a few small items of intrigue with which to amuse yourself in idle moments, you should be covered for most situations. If there's room, a rolled-up bag within the bag can come in handy – not least to save the other contents if you find yourself in urgent need of a place to throw up.

Using the City for Exercise

Very little connects you to your city better than using it as your exercise machine. Whether it's parkour, skateboarding, running, cycling, military circuit training, t'ai chi, swimming, yoga, capoeira or plain old walking, being active in your city rather than loafing indoors or travelling in cars, trains and buses has benefits beyond simply upping your heart rate.

Full disclosure: I am not a role model when it comes to fitness. I try, and yet procrastination all too often gets in the way. A friend told me recently that some people run because they love it, but most people run because they love cake. Were I to run at all I would fall into the latter camp, for sure.

But given the chance, time and weather, I would walk everywhere if I could. Walking allows me to observe and think at the same time. Just as getting lost heightens your instincts, so walking gives you a sharp awareness of your environment. The mechanized rhythm of putting one foot in front of the other can act as a catalyst for processing thoughts, too. It is therapeutic; brain and body are engaged in unison. The nineteenth-century Danish philosopher Søren Kierkegaard shared my love, though he expressed it slightly better:

> Above all do not lose your desire to walk. Every day I walk myself into a state of well-being and walk away from every illness. I have walked myself into my best thoughts, and I know of no thought so burdensome that one cannot walk away from it. But by sitting still, and the more one sits still,

the closer one comes to feeling ill. Thus if one just keeps walking, everything will be all right.

Cycling is the urban exercise–transport hybrid of our times. A pack of cyclists sailing through a sunny urban setting is the very picture of a happy, healthy city. My first-hand experience of cycling is limited, but those bitten by the bug have told me it is like being in a hypnotic state; you can have the same song or a single line going round to the rhythm of your pedals and, far from driving you insane, it feels like barely a moment has passed from boarding your bike to disembarking at the other end. It's euphoric. You feel acutely connected to your environment, urban and climate. As cyclists gain in number, so too are authorities compelled to accommodate them and provide for them safely. The upsurge in urban cycling is beneficial for the health of any city, whether you're on the saddle yourself or not. Bikes do not have exhausts.

Exercising in the city can mean working with and against its often brutal built environment (think skateboarding or parkour). At the other end of the spectrum it can mean being enveloped by its more natural pockets. Swimming in the city is a magical thing: be it a brisk dip in London's post-war lidos, an afternoon bobbing in Copenhagen's harbour baths, floating round Bern in the strong current of the river Aare, or plunging into the Baltic outside the Sauna Society in Helsinki's suburbs. Being in water in the city is a calming experience. It feels incredibly natural to find yourself in a suspended, womb-like state in such an unnatural, man-made environment.

Can I join in?

5. How to Give Back and Grow

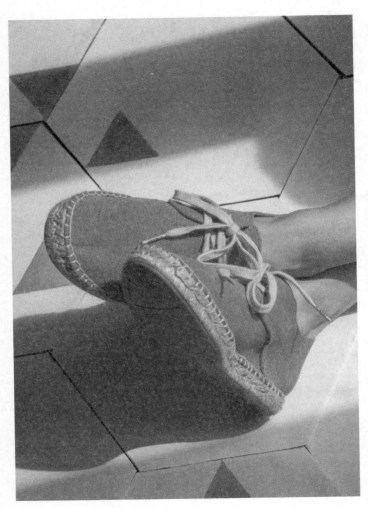

Am I part of the city?

'There is no such thing as a boring place.'
(JONATHAN MEADES, *MUSEUM WITHOUT WALLS*)

Cities are living organisms. It is easy to assume that it's the responsibility of a mayor's office or local council to keep a city healthy, and in many official capacities this is certainly the case when it comes to cultivating public space and amenities. But there is a far greater part of urban life that requires ordinary city dwellers to take responsibility for our habitat, to feed it properly and to keep it alive. Apathy and neglect turn streets into grim and scary places. It's incredible how our animal senses can quickly pick up on an unhappy environment, raising hairs on the backs of our necks. It is important to care not only for our immediate urban surroundings but also, as we've already touched upon, for our fellow citizens and for the city as a whole. It is important to appreciate your place and your actions in the bigger picture; to understand the effect and the power of the micro on the macro; to see the wood and the trees together. It is important to have perspective.

Find Your Voice and Make It Heard

How do you fit into your city? Are you an active part of it? What do you give to it? Where is your voice heard? As urban dwellers, we are the cells that combine to make an organism. We have power and energy as individual cells, and it is good to feel that power and harness it in a positive way. You do not have to work in the mayor's office to effect change. You can make your voice heard in a city in smaller but no less significant ways.

When people talk of feeling drowned by urban life, they describe ways in which the city has got the better of them. It defeats them and they are exhausted from fighting it. Knowing your individual place in the city and having a voice within it is a way of keeping your head above water and not being sucked under. To stand up and be counted is to feel alive. Many of the lessons learnt from previous chapters are crucial here: keeping a routine, staying conscious, establishing a network of small acquaintances, making time for people who make you feel good, carving out regular space for yourself to do something just for you. These are all tools for city living that make you feel in control.

Once you have the strength and energy that come from feeling in control, you will no doubt feel like you are thriving in your city. Then it is your responsibility to give back, to speak up and to play an active part. Friends of mine have done all manner of things: from starting a Greek food stall ('I Should Be Souvlaki', I kid you not) to starting a walking book club that combines talking with walking in a location pertinent to the book they have read. One friend set up a gallery and annual rooftop sculpture commission in a car park in a part of London that has subsequently spawned a large art scene and regeneration of the local area in its wake. Today it is not difficult to make an idea a reality, to find empty places and people to fill them, to create culture. We all have the tools to shape culture to some degree, by organizing, attending and spreading the word. We can all create or contribute to experiences that touch other inhabitants, and this feels good. You don't have to start a gallery or spend your weekends carving kebab meat, but consider what your strengths and interests might be and how you can give something of yourself to others, something of yourself to your city.

'I shall leave the city not less, but greater, better and more beautiful than when I found it.' There is much to consider in this extract from the Ephebic Oath, sworn by young men in Classical Athens on becoming a citizen. Classical Athens wasn't just the birthplace of democracy – it also spawned, through Plutarch, Thucydides, Socrates, Plato and Aristotle (to name some of its more famous minds), a vast canon of philosophy that underpins what the city represents. What connects their discourse is the thread that we, as citizens, have a duty and a responsibility to respect the city as an entity greater than the sum of its parts.

Join a March

Just as the grim rush-hour surge can make you weep for humankind, so joining a march can restore your faith in humanity enormously. People have marched in cities since time began. It is a powerful signifier of democracy, and a symbolic tool to make feelings visible. The experience of bodies walking together for a common cause makes you acutely aware of your place and power as an individual.

At the same time, it makes you aware of your importance as a tiny part of something much bigger, with a voice that has the power to change things. It makes you feel active and alive. One of the most striking moments in Gus Van Sant's 2008 film *Milk* (about the life of gay rights activist Harvey Milk) is when Milk advises the police in San Francisco, trying to keep order in front of a riotous swell of activists, to 'let them march'. It is a method of group expression, a basic right and a way of making a collective voice heard. It is a show of solidarity – your shared belief is strong enough to bring you to the streets. It is an emotional, rousing, exhilarating, important feeling to experience.

Dictate Your Own Experience

At a time when the horrors we see in the news make it easy to be scared, it's more important than ever to be intrepid. There is no denying terrorism is a real threat, in some cities more than others. But, as we have heard from many world leaders, if we change our behaviour in any way to accommodate the fear of 'what if?', then terrorism is winning.

A recent artwork by the British artist Richard Wentworth (commissioned by Transport for London) asked people the simple question: 'If history could be folded, where would you put the crease?' I passed it twice every day for months, and I don't think I'd be alone in answering September 11th, 2001. It's difficult to overestimate the rippling effects of that day on our lives, and it's hard to imagine the repercussions subsiding. I believe the way we feel about life changed that day, culturally, politically, socially and economically.

Four years later, on July 7th 2005, the London transport system was attacked. As I walked back home that morning after the underground network spat all commuters out onto the streets, my feelings were difficult to process. Official information was slow to emerge, but rumours were rife. Absorbing such unnatural events in real time is impossible. We are incapable of taking in such a tidal wave of facts and emotions all at once. For the lucky majority of us not directly caught up in the horrors, it was a day of suspended reality; I remember lying in bed that night asking myself how I felt, and not being able to answer. I was oddly numb. Helpless. Not even scared – angry or defiant at that stage.

The next day I went to work. I'd love to claim that this was an act of defiance, but the truth is I was going on holiday for a fortnight the day after, and there were things that needed to happen for me to be able to detach. It was an eerie sensation travelling in London that day. There was fear in the air, of course, but it was strength and solidarity that were the overriding feelings. People were alert. They looked out for one another. Deliberations of 'should we or shouldn't we be out and about?' were met with the stoic response of getting on with it, 'else they've won'. We had all heard our grandparents and parents talk of British stoicism, wartime spirit and stiff upper lips, but for many of us this was the first time we'd experienced it first-hand.

Ten years on, I asked my friends whether they ever feel scared or threatened in the city. One gave the following response, which I find moving, beautifully expressed and utterly sensible:

I have never felt scared. Not even after the 7th July bombings. I didn't feel weird, even. I'm not very fatalistic but I am certain that I want to lead my life the way I lead it and not have that dictated to me by someone else's actions or threats.

I can't control every aspect of what will happen to me every day when I shut the door to my house behind me and go out into the big world. I have to take tubes. I have to take buses. Hopefully I'm not on one with someone who wants to detonate a bomb. I'm not going to let that thought ever stop me from doing something.

We all take our own lives into our hands every day, and who knows when our time will come? We cannot and must not live in fear. Be in charge of your life and the experiences you have. Be alert still, but don't be paranoid to the point of paralysis. Be intrepid. We'd do well to live by those sage words immortalized by Wieden + Kennedy for Nike: 'Just Do It'.

Be a Tourist in Your Own City

Nobody wants to feel like a tourist, not even tourists themselves. 'Touristy' has negative connotations. A tourist trap is a bad place to find yourself. Being on the tourist trail implies that you lack the imagination to look beyond a guidebook. Checking a guidebook in public singles you out as a tourist, reliant on a writer to tell you where to go rather than using your own judgement. It's too easy to be snobbish about tourism.

But there are many lessons to be learnt from being a tourist in the place you call home. It's shocking how many of us have not 'seen the sights' in our own cities. Whether it's the palace, the parliament, the natural history museum, the observatory, the boat trips,

Can I see my house from here?

the botanical gardens, the iconic building, the photogenic monument or the classic sunset spot, these are dots on a map, chapters in a guidebook and stops on a tour for good reason. They represent the history and the culture of the place in which we live. They form the lens through which others see and experience our city – and the more ways we can look at our city, the more interesting it becomes.

Tourist spots might not have the grit and gristle of the more interesting subculture that we would prefer to spend time and money exploring. They might be a million miles away from the reality of our urban experience. But they are the story of our city's past and its present, and it would be arrogant not to embrace the mainstream, the renowned and the famous to some degree. Every city is rich with stories and experiences, and sometimes we shun the best ones simply because we assume we know them already. A humbler approach will open a whole new world for you. Take a seat on an open-topped sightseeing bus with the school groups, and I guarantee you will learn things you never knew. Have tea at that landmark hotel you've always scoffed at and go for cocktails at the top of the tallest building. Naff? Ironic? No, probably just fun.

Being a tourist in your own city opens your eyes in a different way to the place you live: to its story, its history, its present and the way others see it. If someone asked you to curate a tour of places that give an honest slice of what your city is like, it's unlikely you'd point them to the tourist destinations. We are guilty of assuming they have been Disneyfied, that the stories they tell are sugar-coated or commercially driven and no longer honest. Give them a chance still. Buckingham Palace is insanely weird, and likely to lodge itself in your memory for far longer than an afternoon of doing errands or going shopping. The London Eye might be sponsored by Coca-Cola, but it still has the best views of the city and beyond.

It's not just about the attractions or sites, though. Take the tourist approach and explore the city beyond your routine patch and comfort zones. Go to the stops at the end of the line. Get to know parks on the other side of town. Go for walks in the suburbs. Try the institutional and the brand-new restaurants and bars. I've written frequently about the importance of being active and plugged in to your city. Being a tourist in it is one of the best ways of doing this. It means you are taking an interest in your city. You are opening yourself up to it. You are learning about its past and present. You are observing it, experiencing it, taking from it and giving back to it.

The Value of Leaving the City

*'And those who were seen dancing were thought to be
crazy by those who could not hear the music.'*
(Friedrich Nietzsche)

I have not shied away from the fact that urban living is a slog, and it would be unrealistic to pretend that all of its challenges can be overcome by a pneumatic cheeriness. It is a requirement for your sanity that you build in regular trips away from the city. We all need breaks from our day-to-day lives, regardless of where we live. No matter how wonderful our lot in life, I think we've all felt a sense of yearning to be on board as we watch an aeroplane in the sky above.

There is a certain thrill in the air at big urban train termini; the same can be said about airports. It is the tension of waiting for people to arrive and the emotion wrapped up in imminent farewells; the excitement of a long-awaited break about to begin, and the deflation of a holiday of a lifetime just finished. These feelings fill the air and it's impossible not to pick up on them. I have a friend who worked near Gatwick airport, south of London, as part of her training at a marketing firm. At the start and close of every day she would get on the train to the airport and cross it to catch a shuttle bus to her office. Twice daily she would be surrounded by the energy of the people, planes, trains coming and going, without ever leaving or arriving herself. She said it was torture.

Leaving the city requires a surprising amount of effort. The city has a mysterious hold over us that can induce an irrational sense of panic at the prospect of leaving. For all that we know we want a break (and might be looking forward to it), the idea of upheaval and effort required to reacclimatize to city life on return can make us uneasy. The city is often spoken of as a bubble in which people float around, sheltered from life outside. It is precisely for this reason that leaving the city is so important. It gives you a vital sense of perspective.

To my mind, there are three lengths of break: the day trip, the weekend break and the holiday. Each has its own value. Day trips are good for a jolt. They can bring you round to your senses. They can offer an emergency lifeline when problems or anxieties seem insurmountable. They can be riotous fun. They are metaphorical and literal breaths of fresh air. The fact that you can wake up and go to sleep in your own bed but have a day's adventure in between is thrilling. A day trip can both energize you and slow you down. It is a tonic and a treat and something to be cherished, used, indulged in as often as you feel the need. Familiarize yourself with a few good destinations, and you will feel the benefits of investing a little of yourself in them and knowing what they can give you in return. A day trip is an oft-needed, fast reminder that there is a very different life just outside the big smoke.

Weekend breaks, whether within your own country or abroad, are more involved. They are about discovery, but they also have the power to kick-start you out of a malaise. You can achieve a lot of thinking, recharging and exploring in a two- or three-night break. Some of my favourite holidays have been three-night trips with friends to rural cottages in the more barren, dramatic parts of Britain, where we get a train, hire a car and fill it with food and wine, firewood and coal, and lock ourselves away. This sort of self-sufficiency is a good way of reminding yourself what you are capable of.

Longer holidays are what many of us yearn for. Just as lying in bed all day can sometimes be the best thing for you, lying on a beach or by a pool for two weeks with nothing but a sack of suntan cream and a few good books can be lifesaving. It is often hard to recognize or admit when you need a holiday because it requires a degree of objective assessment, which is unfortunately one of the things we find most difficult when we are run down. Most of us need to work holidays into our calendar in advance (though if you've ever had the opportunity to make a last-minute decision and hop on a plane for two weeks at short notice, you'll know how wonderful that can be). A long break during which you can unwind and establish a loose holiday routine is like pressing the pause button on life as you know it. Look at yourself, and ask yourself a few questions. Assess the direction your life is heading in and take stock of what, if anything, you want to change. In among the indulgent food, swimming and the ripping yarns, a long holiday is a good time to reflect and think about life and change.

As well as allowing you to gain perspective on your daily life, breaks are good for another reason: they allow you to fall in love with your city all over again. I'm sure we've all experienced the sadness of coming back from holiday, circling over the grey skies of your city before coming into land. Yet fairly soon that melancholy is replaced by the thrill of excitement as the city rushes to greet you. It can be a wonderful feeling returning to the city, whether you've been away a day, a weekend or a month. It is only on leaving and returning again that you can properly gauge how you feel about living in the city. With any luck you'll be reinvigorated by a break, but if you're struck by a feeling of misery that fails to lift, then it might be time to take action and consider a new life elsewhere.

It's a good idea to write down any feelings and thoughts, ambitions and goals you might have decided on while you were away. It's a way of committing yourself to keeping your relationship with your city moving in the right direction. We all too easily make promises to ourselves on holiday that we will change things back home, and before we know it we've slipped into our lives and forgotten our good intentions. We are, after all, only human.

Conclusion

Do I feel free?

City-bashing has become fashionable. Lately there has been a proliferation of opinion pieces in the press and online about (and by) people leaving the city because life there is too difficult – or because the opportunities we once thought were only available in an urban context are now more widespread. There is no doubt that city living is expensive, stressful and at times difficult, myopic and suffocating; but as I've attempted to show in this book, there's also a great deal of joy to be found in it. Cultivating this joy is the key to leading a happy urban life. In light of all that I've discussed, let's revisit that quote from Jane Jacobs at the start of the book:

'Being human is itself difficult, and therefore all kinds of settlements have problems. Big cities have difficulties in abundance, because they have people in abundance.'

The difficulties we face in city life are difficulties inherent in the human condition, magnified by the proximity of so many other people. How do you live in the city? You hold on to your humanity.

It is my belief that if we start with ourselves and nurture our own sense of contentment, well-being and happiness, then we stand a better chance of spreading this positive feeling to others we come into contact with. Whatever the circumstances city life might throw at us, ultimately each of us holds the keys to our own happiness. We can be radiators or drains, radiating warmth into or draining life from those around us. If cities are to thrive in our time of urban expansion, they require us to bring life, feeling, warmth and energy. They require us to be human.

Homework

The following recommendations are a mixture of books, sources and experiences that I have found helpful, both in everyday life and in the course of research for this book. They are suggestions for digging deeper into some of the ideas covered here. Some relate to specific points I have made, and some are personal – I don't expect everyone to love Madonna's *Ray of Light*, for instance – but I hope there will be something to suit most people's needs and interests.

Introduction

I have already said that this book is intended as a handbook for people living in cities and not as an urbanist tract. That said, some of the greater, more interesting urbanist writers will provide a comprehensive background to the book and the following list forms a rounded group of urbanist thinkers.

The first (and last) quote in the book comes from American author and activist Jane Jacobs, whose seminal book *The Death and Life of Great American Cities* kick-started a human-centred approach to urbanist discourse when it was published in 1961. Her tone is light and urgent, perhaps with a touch of haughtiness. It is as close to bedtime reading as urbanist handbooks get. Dipping in and out of it will open your eyes to patterns of city living, good and bad, which are as relevant today as ever.

Peter Kageyama, founder of the Creative Cities Summit, is the author of an ode to the love affair between people and cities in *For the Love of Cities*. It rises above statistical analysis to engage in the emotional connection we have to our urban environments.

Edward Glaeser's *Triumph of the City: How Our Greatest Invention Makes us Richer, Smarter, Greener, Healthier and Happier* is a broader celebration that takes in historical, cultural, social and economic factors.

The work of Danish urbanist Jan Gehl is compelling, digestible evidence for the need to put the human experience first in creating healthy cities. Two of his books, *Life Between Buildings* and *Cities for People*, make the case clearly with a host of fascinating observations and examples.

1. How to Feel Your City

Opening yourself up to your environment, your habits and feelings is something Ilse Crawford has spent a life promoting. Her latest book, *A Frame For Life*, charts the growth of her thinking through many projects that have come out of her London-based studio. On the subject of 'feeling' environments, Finnish architect and academic Juhani Pallasmaa is a pioneer. His book *The Eyes of the Skin* has shaped my own thoughts and experiences more than almost any other.

British cultural commentator Jonathan Meades is a genius in my eyes. Many of his older programmes are available on YouTube, and a compendium of scripts and articles was published recently in *Museum Without Walls*. People tend to love or hate his singular, outspoken approach, but nobody could argue that he doesn't express a sense of place poetically.

Architecture critic Rowan Moore has been a great influence on me, successfully translating the often lofty language of architecture into accessible terms. His weekly column in the *Observer* tackles important issues within architecture, urbanism and the built environment, engaging the bigger picture of how and why things matter in context. Moore's book *Why We Build* is a riveting collection of personal experiences and wider thinking on the subject of man's relationship with architecture and the built environment. It should be required reading for every architecture student (and architect).

Dan Hill's blog, City of Sound (www.cityofsound.com), is an excellent exploration of life and cities, exploring issues at the intersection of design, media, music and urbanism.

Monocle's radio station posts a weekly hour-long podcast called 'The Urbanist', hosted by Andrew Tuck, the magazine's editor. It celebrates life in cities and what makes life good via human stories from around the world, on a different theme each week.

Moving away from media, I recommend signing up for a walking tour in your city on a subject of your interest. Beyond the umbrella-wielding, out-of-work-actor guides, there are today many exceptional, specialist tours in all cities if you dig around on the internet for a bit. I have been on a graphic signage tour in San Francisco, ghost walks in Edinburgh and food and architecture tours in London, and each has left me with a valuable insight into the city's past and present.

Most cities have a museum dedicated to city life. Pay it a visit to find out more.

On the topic of FOMO, when it comes to keeping abreast of what's on and what's hot, *Time Out* is still a good listings bible for many streams of culture. Blogs and daily newsletters of more underground happenings are helpful, though many of these events can be filled with scenesters in search of the next big thing.

2. How to Conduct Relationships

Armistead Maupin's *Tales of the City* series is a wonderful journey through friendships and romances set in San Francisco, following the same lovable characters over the course of decades. It is funny, charming and atmospheric, and insightful about both its particular setting and the human condition.

As a feel-good pop-culture study of relationships in a city setting, the classic TV sitcom *Friends* still holds up well.

Turning back to non-fiction, *Helsinki Beyond Dreams*, edited by Hella Hernberg, explores human stories from the Finnish capital, bringing to life examples of how the small city is doing many interesting things to raise the quality of life for its inhabitants. Helsinki has a more progressive attitude than most cities towards urban development that puts its inhabitants first. There are many projects and ideas in this book that are relevant for cities around the world and it's the human connections that are repeatedly cited as the source of success.

The small Japanese city of Kagoshima, on the southernmost island of Kyushu, is a similarly fascinating example of a city where neighbourliness is taken seriously in all walks of life, from food to retail to community-organized sweeping of ash from streets (it sits in front of the live volcano of Sakurajima, which routinely puffs ash dust over the city). The Good Neighbours Jamboree is an annual festival that brings its citizens together for a riotous celebration. It is worth co-ordinating a trip there to get to the heart of a city that really works for its people.

Airbnb has transformed the way we can travel and experience cities, principally because it allows for connections with real people in areas that hotels and hostels have not yet penetrated. More than just an accommodation service, the goal is to open up neighbour-hoods and establish real human connections to local life. It's a good way of experiencing 'the real city'.

Places where you can be comfortably alone are many and varied. Benches in parks are good places for slowing down and breathing out. Maybe my Catholic upbringing has something to do with the fact that I find churches soothing for solitude, despite not being reli-gious. The lucky Finns have the Kamppi Chapel of Silence in the heart of Helsinki, which is a breathtakingly beautiful windowless, curved wooden box perfect for stepping into to press pause on your life. There should be one in every city. Until then, a good pair of noise-cancelling headphones can help to occasionally block out the clamour of city life.

There are an increasing number of books, TV shows and films dedicated to the near-future depiction of how our reliance on tech-nology might spiral into a not-so-nice world. Charlie Brooker's *Black Mirror* TV series is a collection of new realities that are disturbing and entertaining in equal measure. Jacob Silverman's book *Terms of Service: Social Media and the Price of Constant Connection* will be enough to have you shut down your Facebook and Twitter feeds. Dave Eggers' *The Circle* is a fun read that leaves you with a lingering sense of unease that we are perhaps already living in the world he has portrayed. Margaret Atwood's genius novel *The Heart Goes Last* brings wit and horror together, the former helping us to stomach the latter.

3. How to Be Hard and Soft

Ayn Rand's seminal tome *The Fountainhead* is a weighty but brilliant dissection of working life in the city, told through the contrasting fates of two architects in mid-twentieth-century New York.

French writer Georges Perec's essay 'Species of Spaces' is a more abstract expression of thinking about space, how we move through it and experience it. It will open your eyes and mind to a new way of thinking about (and looking at) life in the city. Italo Calvino's *Invisible Cities* is almost poetry rather than prose, but his descriptions of imaginary cities, told by Marco Polo to his host Kublai Khan, are mesmerizing and beautiful.

The paintings of L.S. Lowry are deeply evocative depictions of work in the city. His main subject was industrial life in the hard cities of northern England. His famous matchstick crowds, heads down, milling in and out of factories along hard cobbled streets are a humbling reminder of a time before the concept of work/life balance entered our consciousness. They are dark and disturbing.

The writings of Matthew Crawford are good for perspective on work and life and how we can embed better values in both. I'd recommend *The Case for Working with Your Hands* and the more recent *The World Beyond Your Head*.

If you feel you are veering into danger territory of alcohol or substance abuse or addiction, Alcoholics Anonymous and Narcotics Anonymous have worldwide networks and open doors of support.

4. How to Move and Be Still

It is always fascinating to take public transport in cities you visit to understand how different cities cope with the same conundrum of keeping their populations fluid. My favourite experiences of moving in cities are taking the extraordinarily efficient subway system in Tokyo; travelling by tram in San Francisco, where the city's vertiginous topography makes it feel like a fairground; and chugging along the backstreet canals of Venice in the vaporetto buses or water taxis (beware the cost of the latter!).

Walking is made infinitely more pleasurable if you have a comfortable pair of shoes. Trainers are no longer associated with only teenagers and most big brands have started going beyond fashion to ensure they kit you out with a pair that suits the shape of your feet and the way that you walk or run.

To engage with your senses, investigate the work of Norwegian odour artist Sissel Tolaas, who has devoted her life to reawakening our sense of smell, including mapping the smells of different city districts the world over.

Finding music to suit your given mood and pace is deeply personal, but it's a helpful tool to build a library to suit different speeds. You don't need me to tell you that music can transport you and I'm currently being transported by Danish singer-songwriter Agnes Obel (two albums, *Philharmonics* and *Aventine*) in my more thoughtful, slow days. And for nostalgia's sake I'm enjoying revisiting Madonna and William Orbit's excellent *Ray of Light* album. Listening to the title track while walking through a crowd at rush hour is invigorating.

The Citymapper app is a requirement if you want to be as efficient as possible in getting from A to B, and is available in an increasing number of cities around the world. If you live in a city that is not covered, Google Maps is still a handy tool.

When it comes to exercise, the internet is your friend for finding local groups, recommended routes, clubs and swimming spots. Cyclists should seek out Rapha's collection of city cycling guides or the beautiful collection of European guides, *City Cycling Europe*, by Andrew Edwards and Max Leonard.

5. How to Give Back and Grow

The Venice Architecture Biennale is a good place to head for a sense of current crises in city life, as well future solutions. Breadth of experience and information on what's happening in other cities can be found in *Monocle* magazine. I may be biased as a former employee, but I think it takes a refreshing approach to urban coverage, writing about cities from a human perspective, highlighting the experience of living there and shining a light on places you'd struggle to find in other titles. It has been instrumental in dragging the topic of urban quality of life from the sidelines into the mainstream.

The Sunday Assembly is a quickly growing secular gathering in community spaces around the world. It mixes culture, comedy, pop music and discussion under the tagline 'Live Better, Help Often, Wonder More' and manages to steer clear of being saccharine (www.sundayassembly.com).

If you are willing to follow people at the forefront of their fields that you don't personally know, then Instagram can be a helpful tool for feeling connected to your city. It functions as a twenty-first-century photographic mapping system: you can see into other people's lives and experiences and, in turn, share your own. It's not as sinister as it sounds. Thanks to Instagram I have found all sorts of things out about London and all it has to offer that I would otherwise never have come across, from where to buy the ultimate ice-cream-and-cookie sandwich, to undiscovered architectural gems in the far reaches of the city.

If you want to give back in a more physical way, investigate bringing Greenbird to your city. It was born in Tokyo, but is gradually spreading its wings around the world (though currently only in Colombo, Paris and Anaheim). It is a volunteer litter-collection service, more like a club than a chore, with the motto 'A clean town also makes people's hearts and minds clean'.

Finally, for escaping the city, I find One Off Places a useful source of very nice little houses to stay in in rural areas (www.oneoffplaces.com). Its charm lies in the lack of identikit holiday rental home furnishing; in most cases the personality and character of the owner is evident.

Did I lock the front door?

Acknowledgements

I'd like to thank the brilliant photographer Ana Cuba for bringing to life so many of the feelings I've written about in her beautiful photographs that accompany the book.

I owe a great deal to my former employers and mentors at various jobs: Tony, Vanita, Alex, Tyler, Andrew and Ilse, who have each shaped and nurtured my thinking and have (often) allowed me to express my own views.

Thank you to Morgwn and The School of Life for having faith that I could take on this project and thank you to Cindy, Zennor, Laura, Charlotte and Robin at Pan Macmillan for steering the book (and me) through its various stages with invaluable criticism and patience.

I have relied upon the insight and experience of many friends in my research and special thanks goes to those who contributed, questioned and opened up: May, Charlie, Alex, Emily Smith and Emily London, James, Hannah, Ed, Fred and Mike.

Permissions Acknowledgements

Notes

Notes

Notes

Notes

Notes

Notes

TOOLS FOR THINKING

A RANGE OF THOUGHTFUL STATIONERY, GAMES
& GIFTS FROM THE SCHOOL OF LIFE

Good thinking requires good tools. To complement our classes, books and therapies, THE SCHOOL OF LIFE now offers a range of stationery, games and gifts that are both highly useful and stimulating for the eye and mind.

THESCHOOLOFLIFE.COM

If you enjoyed this book, we'd encourage you to check out
other titles in the series:

If you'd like to explore more good ideas from everyday life,
THE SCHOOL OF LIFE runs a regular programme of classes, workshops,
and special events in London and other cities around the world.

THESCHOOLOFLIFE.COM